Bob Reeser

1406

Enlightened Cherishing

An Essay on Aesthetic Education

Enlightened Cherishing

An Essay on Aesthetic Education

THE 1972 KAPPA DELTA PI LECTURE

by Harry S. Broudy

PROFESSOR OF PHILOSOPHY OF EDUCATION

UNIVERSITY OF ILLINOIS

Published for Kappa Delta Pi by

UNIVERSITY OF ILLINOIS PRESS

URBANA, CHICAGO, LONDON

Permission to reprint lines from "Sailing to Byzantium" from William
Butler Yeats, *Collected Poems,* has been granted by the Macmillan Com-
pany (copyright 1928 by the Macmillan Company, renewed 1956 by
Georgie Yeats).

Contents

Enlightened Cherishing

An Essay on Aesthetic Education

I

Enlightened Cherishing

WHEN a society is ailing, its institutions ache, but when it is no longer aware of its ailments, it is very near death. Accordingly, while the barrage of criticism directed against the public schools in recent years can be construed as part of the general criticism to which all our institutions are being subjected, it is a good omen for the health of our schools that they are very conscious of the complaints voiced about them. The criticisms are of various sorts, however, and part of educational wisdom is to respond to them selectively.

First of all, it is well to distinguish criticism of *education* from that directed at *schooling*. When, for example, Socrates, or Plato speaking through Socrates, criticized education in the *Republic,* he was attacking the total value system of the Athenians. He was saying that Athens should be governed by a small class of men who could be trained to achieve a glimpse of the absolute forms of truth, goodness, and beauty and who could discipline themselves to use this insight for the benefit of the body politic. This meant that Athens should not be governed by the mass of the people casting votes on affairs of state about which many of them, he believed, knew nothing. The training of the guardians would involve a radical departure from the curriculum of both elementary and higher schooling, but the changes he proposed were more

3

than changes in school practice. When, for example, he denounced the myths and poetry being taught to the young, he was criticizing the theology of the conventional Athenian religion; he was criticizing an uncritical tradition more than the schools which were perpetuating it. Similarly, when he counseled that the guardians study geometry and music as highly theoretical subjects, this was a radical proposal, but it had more to do with a theory of knowledge and reality than with the current school's teaching of arithmetical computation.

There is a type of criticism that indicts the schooling of an age because it seems to serve success routes of which the critic does not approve. Thus in recent years social critics who condemned the materialism of our times — the desire for bigger automobiles and larger television sets — and the feverish pursuit of personal gratification assailed the schools for reinforcing these tendencies. Those critics, on the other hand, who thought the American middle class was unduly preoccupied with the Puritan ethic — as manifested by repression of sexual desires and timidity about changing the mores of clothing and hairiness — castigated the schools for oppressing the children and robbing them of their freedom and spontaneity. Middle-class schools, they said, were joyless dungeons devised by dour Puritans for keeping down the young, the poor, and the blacks. Or, as one apostle of the new hot humanism put it, the schools were enemies of the young. This type of criticism is one way of announcing that the body politic is aching all over and that the school is contributing to the general illness.

At the other end of the scale criticism was directed toward the school's methods of instruction, e.g., in reading or arithmetic, or to the graded classroom, or to methods of discipline, or to bussing and homework. To remedy these alleged shortcomings, the critics suggested very specific changes: the nongraded classroom, movable furniture, and new techniques for reading instruction.

Both types of criticisms, insofar as they point to some genuine

4

source of discomfort or inefficiency, are beyond criticism. The trouble arises when they confront each other. Or, more correctly, because they never quite confront each other; not traveling on the same level — like automobiles that pass each other on a clover-leaf intersection — they pass each other but never meet. To the global critic, the educationist's prescriptions smack of giving aspirin tablets to cure a national neurosis; to the minute critic of school practice, the global critic seems to be saying something important but something that ought to be addressed to the home, the church, and the Congress rather than the school.

One type of criticism, however, falls somewhere between these two extremes. It is concerned with what is variously called value education, character education, or moral education. Both the school and the larger society are involved with it and have a role in it. Nobody downgrades the importance of value education, and nobody would argue that either the school or the social order has done as well with it as one would like. Moreover, value education can be and is discussed on as general a level as the national character and destiny and on as specific a level as the curriculum materials and methods that the school might use to discharge its part of the obligation. The resulting Babel is stimulating but confusing.

In this essay we shall be dealing with a very old form of the question, already raised by Socrates in the *Protagoras* and the *Meno,* Can virtue be taught? To which we may add some sub-questions also raised by Socrates: If virtue can be taught, is it a special kind of knowledge of which there can be specialists? If so, who are the specialists? What are the norms by which the good is to be judged? What is the source of these norms? Why do men who know the good and say they are committed to it nevertheless fail to act in accordance with their knowledge and commitments?

I shall not try to explore all of these questions. On the contrary, the essay will concentrate on a special form of the last question: Why do men fail to act in accordance with their acknowledged norms, even though school and society have done rather well in habituating them to the mores of the group, and the principles of right conduct and choice have been drilled into their consciousness and vocabulary since infancy? Or, as the title of the lecture indicates, what sort of schooling might lead to enlightened cherishing?

Obviously there would be no problem if the kind of knowledge that was needed for virtue was like the knowledge of mathematics or physics or history. It was easy to teach the slave boy in the *Meno* geometry, but one could not be sure that the sons of Pericles and other famous men, despite the best of schooling, could or would learn to be virtuous.[1] One commentator, puzzling over the peculiar sort of knowledge that could be equated with virtue, hazarded the opinion that "if a man has knowledge of what is virtuous and *also* knowledge that it is always better for one to do what is virtuous, then he will always (so long as he has this knowledge and virtuous behavior in his power) behave virtuously."[2] This kind of knowledge is more akin to dedication and cherishing than to the assertion of true propositions.

Cherishing is a special kind of love and desire. It is not merely a desire for possession of the object but, rather, a desire to preserve and care for the object because it has properties that delight us, i.e., properties intrinsically valuable. *Enlightened cherishing* can be thought of as a love of objects and actions that by certain norms and standards are worthy of our love. It is a love that knowledge justifies. Unlike the love of a mother for the black sheep, enlightened cherishing is passionate but not blind. Without this love of the best, value experience suffers from two defects. One is servitude to blind or capricious impulse and desire. The other is the joyless, routinized discharge of conventional obliga-

[1] An observation by F. J. Woodbridge in his essay on the *Meno* in Alexander Sesonske and Noel Fleming, *Plato's Meno* (Belmont, Calif.: Wadsworth Publishing Co., 1965), p. 59.

[2] *Ibid.*

6

tions whose "rightness" lies less in the nature of the tasks they command than in the general expectation that they will be carried out. Neither defect is compatible with enlightened cherishing.

The schools and the community conspire to habituate us to value choices and exhort us to abide by certain ideals to which the community gives vigorous lip service. However, since these approaches have never achieved the kind of enlightened cherishing that is the real goal of value education, one begins to suspect that we may have overlooked another dimension of value experience. I shall call it the aesthetic dimension, which, although in many ways the most potent factor in our value experience, has received the least attention in our schools.

VALUE EXPERIENCE: STANDARDS AND MOTIVES

When we complain about the values espoused by a person, a generation, or a people and are challenged to give reasons for our disapproval, we point to the violation of some norm we consider valid, or we say that the person acted from an improper motive, or both. If, for example, we disapprove of a fifteen-year-old smoking marijuana, our reasoning would probably run something like this: the community disapproves and the law forbids the use of marijuana, and it is bad for the health. Thus three standards we regard as valid have been violated.

But we might go further and say, "We realize that for a fifteen-year-old to break the conventions with regard to marijuana is not a disaster. He will outgrow his indifference to the expectations of the neighbors and the dictates of the law. And a little marijuana will not necessarily ruin his health. What really bothers us is that he acted from a questionable motive: a desire to gratify his senses, a desire to do what others were doing, idle curiosity, perhaps even a desire to revenge himself on his parents. The results of the marijuana may not have lasting evil consequences, but yielding to this kind of motivation will, because it will become

7

part of his character, his personality, and no good can come from such a character."

Whether the values chosen are in the fields of economic activity, recreation, friendship, or civic obligations or in the realms of truth, morality, religion, or art, good choosing involves adherence to a valid standard — the highest one that is applicable to the situation — and adherence from the right motive — the highest applicable one. And these two classes of requirements define the sphere of value education. Of any scheme of value education we can properly ask: What norms of conduct is it inculcating, and to what extent is a desire to meet that norm part of the motivation of conduct?

The most familiar norm is the expectation of our reference group, the group whose opinion about our conduct we respect. "What will people say?" sums up this norm, and if you can specify the people you have in mind, you will also identify the reference group in question. A cut above this norm is the expectation of the law, which formalizes the mores or expectations of the group. I shall not go into the reasons for regarding these expectations as important and valid. Some of these reasons are lost in the remote history of the group so that all that is left is a custom for which the rationale is no longer apparent. For example, our neighbors in the suburbs expect us to favor them with a smoothly barbered expanse of lawn in front of our house. Perhaps there was some practical reason for it at one time, but it is hard to guess what it could have been. Yet not to mow the lawn with weekly devotion would earn us hostile stares, if not a visit from a committee. The motive which actuates us to do what people expect us to do is fear or at least some anxiety lest we earn their disapproval and hostility.

This does not sound like a very lofty standard and neither does the motivation. Yet it is perhaps the most powerful of our motives and the most ubiquitous of our standards. As a matter of fact, the vast majority of parents would be happy to settle for

8

social conformity and no more. If the school could assure mothers and fathers that their children would behave as the community expected them to, and that their sons and daughters would be properly anxious to please that community, parents would be more than satisfied. It would mean that chances would be very good that their offspring would not get into serious trouble. Parents might not want to say that this is *all* that happiness means, but they would regard everyone else but themselves as happy who managed to stay out of hospitals, jail, the divorce courts, and unusually large debt. Fiction, movies, and other art forms, of course, have little trouble showing how unhappy such conforming people can be, because, as we shall see, happiness presupposes certain aesthetic conditions as well as physiological and social ones. Tension, suspense, surprise, and drama are needed for the kind of absorption in life that happiness requires. Simply staying out of trouble reduces fear and anxiety, but it increases boredom, and nobody equates happiness with boredom.

The conformity solution is so eminently sensible that sages in every age have wondered why some people a great deal of the time, and all people some of the time, kick over the traces and defy the expectations of the group. The simple answer is that individual men's desires for gratification overcome the restraints imposed by the community (based on average levels of tolerance) so that on occasion one drinks more than is respectable, carries on with extramarital partners, cheats in business, and disobeys the traffic laws. This occasional breaking of rules is so common that the community tacitly operates on a double standard — a collective one that it professes and another that it will tolerate in individuals, if they do not flaunt their indiscretions. The school, however, operates on a single standard, the professed one; it will not tolerate in individuals what is forbidden to the group.

But this simple answer is not wholly satisfactory. For men — the same men who disobey laws and social expectations — also acknowledge standards much more demanding than those which their reference groups impose on their members. They can conceive of human beings acting from motives that they would not dream of attributing to other members of the animal kingdom. We shall have to explore this phenomenon because much of what we call value experience is a product of man's imagination both in the expectations he erects and in the means of fulfilling them that he invents.

IMAGINATION

It is worthwhile to dwell on the imagination, especially because we hear very little about it in educational discussion. Imagination is linked somehow to creativity, originality, or spontaneity, and in recent years the word "imaginative" has become an honorific tag for whatever educational reformers happen to advocate. Although imagination is regarded as generally good, and one encounters such phrases as "developing the imagination" and "stimulating the imagination" in educational literature, one is hard put to find much on deliberately using schoolwork for these purposes. It is taken for granted that the arts, especially drama and fiction, have something to do with stimulating the imagination, but when one turns to the literature on art education, one finds little that explicitly discusses the role of the imagination either in life or in art. This cavalier attitude toward the imagination may be partly responsible for the indifferent success the school has had in value education.

If we can imagine the human species deprived of imagination, what would be peculiarly human about it? Physiologically, we are not very different from other species. We have the same sort of physiological drives to food, sex, comfort. We share fear, anger, excitement with the higher animals. We do not differ from them significantly in our reflexive reactions to stimuli that threaten the safety of the organism. If there are instincts, there is a set that is fairly common to large segments of the animal kingdom.

The classic differentia of the human species has been reason:

man is defined as a rational animal, although he has also been characterized as a laughing animal and a featherless biped. But without the ability to imagine, that is, to bring before the mind an image of what is not physically present, we would not be able to reason at all, and not inclined to laugh either. Take, for example, our reasoning in mathematics or logic. What makes it possible for us to reason that if $2 + 2 = 4$, then $4 + 4 = 8$, or to infer that if all men are mortal and if Socrates is a man, that Socrates will die? At some point in our experience the *idea* of number must arise, and such an idea arises only after we can imagine "twoness" apart from particular pairs of things and only after we can compare in imagination the relation between $2 + 2$ and $4 + 4$. Particular physical objects, the tables and chairs around us, are not clothed in envelopes of ideas that we strip off for purposes of thinking about them. We have to imagine particulars so clothed and stripped; we called this mental operation abstraction. All reasoning is done with and through concepts, ideas, notions, and all of these are rooted in an act of imagination which enables us to deal with images and other tokens of actual things rather than with the things themselves. The pride of intellectualism often makes us forget its nonintellectual origins.

In no other department of experience is imagination more potent than in that of desire. Physiologically, so far as our tissues are concerned, when a drive to some gratification is sated, the drive subsides and the organism turns to other business until it is again prodded into life by a recurrence of tissue need. Not so for the human animal. The pleasure of gratification can be separated in imagination from the particular occasion of its occurrence. If eating one ice-cream cone gives pleasure, a boy can imagine the pleasures derived from eating one hundred ice-cream cones. Similarly with our desires for sex, money, comfort, and praise — there is no limit to what our imagination can paint as desirable, and the amount has little to do with how much food, money, or sex our physiological or psychological welfare might require. And, of course, the same imaginative exfoliation of experience magnifies our grief and pain as well. We live in the lands of what might be and what might have been, worlds that for our experience are far greater in volume and import than the world of what now *is*. The same imagination that transforms lust into love and romance can conjure up the fantasies of sexual delights and perversions which, according to current novelists and movie makers, dominate the lives of American men and women. Imagination turns the need for shelter into a construction industry replete with interior decorators and landscape architects. It is imagination that converts food-taking into dining, but it also turns some men into gluttons. By virtue of imagination human life oscillates above and below a vague median line of what we might call natural animality. It soars above it in ideals, science, art, and religion; it drops below it in crimes, cruelties, injustices, and perversions.

We are caught in a dilemma as old as humanity itself. If we restrict desire to what our tissues and health require, then, given a moderately favorable physical environment, our species could lead a healthy animal life. But then what would become of its mental and spiritual life? If, on the other hand, we let our imagination loose to create and roam in the world of what might be, then our desires will lose their natural health. The answer to the dilemma has been a struggle to sort out "natural" desires from those that develop by our imagination, and out of this struggle emerged the question of value standards: How shall we shape our desires? How shall we maximize the power of imagination and yet retain physical and spiritual health?

This is also the goal of value education, and a first approximation is the conventional morality of the group. The mores of the group represent the congealed imagination of the past. Since the group has survived, these mores have a presumptive survival value, but the imagination which produced the mores in the first place restlessly created new possibilities, even while our reflection was rooting out inconsistencies in the mores and gross discrepancies with the changing conditions of life. William Graham Sumner in his *Folkways* rightly celebrated the stabilizing power of mores, but he attributed changes in them to changes in life conditions and imperfect transmission of the mores from one generation to another. Sumner failed to appreciate the dynamism of the imagination. Even if conditions did not change very much, the goods enjoyed by the group and the evils that threatened them would swell beyond reality in imagination; for there is no way for the imagination to limit itself once it embarks on magnification. The strong bull is imagined to give way to a stronger one and he, in turn, to an even more powerful one . . . but why stop? Why not go on to imagine the great bull god, more powerful than any conceivable bull?

The world of actuality, insofar as that world is the work of the human mind and hand, is imagination's legacy. Out of this legacy each individual and each generation can by imagination create possibilities which, if actualized, change the world and enlarge the legacy for future generations.

The very idea of value is a product of imagination. Value is either instrumental or intrinsic (although some objects have both). For anything to have instrumental value it must be thought of as able to help bring about a state of affairs not yet in existence but which thought can entertain. If the thing is to have intrinsic value, it must be valued for itself alone, regardless of its usefulness (if any) for anything else. But what a feat of imagination is required to think of something as desired for itself alone! To do so means to concentrate on an object, e.g., the bloom or fragrance of a rose, without taking account of its relationship to other things.

This is an act of abstraction whereby we imagine the bloom or the fragrance of the rose as if it were a self-sustaining entity about which no further questions need be asked. Yet ordinary life, made up as it is of one transaction with reality after another, rarely permits us the luxury of ignoring the relations of things, because action to be effective must take accurate account of how things and events are connected to each other. It is only with the help of imagination that we can get away from everything but the bloom of the rose early in the morning. Some people whose imagination is not overly active have trouble separating the bloom of the rose from the compost heap which furnished the nutrition for the rose bush.

When we speak of value standards, we are not speaking of meter sticks and weighing scales. Rather, we are comparing an act or an object with an ideal that imagination has extrapolated upon those properties — whether they be of apples, good deeds, or prize cattle — that we have found desirable. To talk of systems of value or of value hierarchies is to talk of a joint product of imagination and classification. The human mind is no more and no less than the operations by which it creates, stores, retrieves, and combines the imagic surrogates of the real world.

In what does human freedom consist if not in the possibility that our experience can move beyond the limits of the here and now? It would never occur to an animal to think of determining itself; the frantic thrashing of an animal in sudden captivity is a reflex response, a desire to be free from its bonds, but not from constraint in general. It takes imagination to think of being free in the sense of issuing commands to oneself.

If I seem to have overemphasized imagination, it is because schools have given their primary attention to the intellectual operations of the mind, especially those of acquiring facts and of problem-solving by hypothetico-deductive thinking. They have done so without realizing that the raw materials for reasoning of all sorts, for idealization and sublimation of physiological drives, for freedom itself, are furnished by the imagination.

The schools are not to be blamed for the relative neglect of imagination, because imagination can run wild; it does not of itself impose limits on the wildness, and not all products of the imagination are creative and constructive. That is why imagination must be disciplined by thought if cherishing is to be enlightened. But as someone has remarked, a boat that is moving can be steered; one that is becalmed cannot. Before there can be disciplined imagination, there must be imagination. Discipline applied to a meager imagination yields little more than ordered sterility.

How does the imagination work? Although this question has fascinated psychologists, philosophers, and artists, we still do not really know. Clearly, images representing experiences of all sorts are somehow retained in the mind — some consciously, some below the level of awareness or, as Lowes put it, in the "thronged yet sleeping subliminal chambers." Some remain almost unchanged, to be recalled vividly and repeatedly — the detail of a wallpaper, for example, that I have not seen for more than fifty years. Others become transformed in storage. Lowes cites an example in which thirty years after reading Oliver Wendell Holmes's *Autocrat at the Breakfast Table* he recalled a passage from it. Holmes had said, "Put an idea in your intelligence and leave it there an hour, a day, a year without ever having occasion to refer to it. When, at last, you return to it, you do not find it as it was when acquired. It has domiciliated itself, so to speak, — become at home, — entered into relation with your other thoughts, and integrated itself with the whole fabric of your mind."[3] But when Lowes recalled this passage, it was in the form of something "germinating and expanding . . . with white and spreading tentacles, like the plant which sprouts beneath a stone. . . ."

What effected this transformation? Was it chance, some "controlling will," some power of intuition groping toward a unified

[3] Quoted in John Livingston Lowes, *The Road to Xanadu: A Study in the Ways of the Imagination* (Boston: Houghton Mifflin, 1927), p. 57.

view of reality?[4] There are all sorts of interesting speculations and reports of artists, scientists, and other creative spirits. There is a general, albeit rough, agreement that after the storing of images in the "thronged yet sleeping subliminal chambers," there comes the "summons which unlocks their secret doors; the pouring up of images linked in new conjunctions provocative of unexpected *aperçus;* the conscious seizing and directing to an end of suggestions which the unconscious operations have supplied."[5]

This description does well enough for the creative act, but for aesthetic education or, rather, for the aesthetic dimension of value education, it is the impressional side of the imagination that is especially important. It takes a well-developed, active imagination to apprehend the creative acts of others when these are objectified in poetry, painting, music, etc.

The ordering or disciplining of the contents of the imagination is done by many factors and agencies. For example, there are the primordial urges to sex and aggression of which the Freudian theory makes so much. According to Freud, when these are repressed, they create a fantasy life of dreams which are acted out in strange ways, ways that evade social disapproval. In the Freudian theory art is a permissible expression of the libidinal urges (especially oedipal ones) that conventional life suppresses. Art is one way of "sublimating" these drives. Whether the Freudian theory is sound or not, it points to the humanizing process whereby physiological needs are transmuted into civilized activities the meanings of which far outrun the original drives. They achieve a quality and life of their own, what Gordon Allport dubbed a "functional autonomy." This new quality can be-

---

[4] For an exhaustive study of these and other aspects of this subject, see Harold Rugg, *Imagination: An Inquiry into the Sources and Conditions That Stimulate Creativity* (New York: Harper and Row, 1963). Of course, the classic work on imagination is still Samuel Taylor Coleridge's *Biographia Literaria.*

[5] Lowes, *The Road to Xanadu,* p. 431.

come more important than the original need, once the culture permits the luxury of going beyond the original need. Dining becomes more important than feeding. Tissue needs, I dare say, are the last thing a hostess at a dinner party thinks about.

Reason exerts another control on the imagination. Science sorts out those creations of the imagination that can stand the scrutiny of logic and empirical inquiry from those that cannot. Science legitimates some of the speculations of science fiction into plausible hypotheses and rejects others as no more than fancy. Reality itself has a sobering effect on the imagination. It brings us back to earth, although sometimes we refuse to come down. Like Walter Mitty, we snap our fingers at reality and carry out the most extraordinary feats in twilight dreams.

We can think of civilization as an index of the efforts of society to control the crude physiological drives of men in the first instance and subsequently to curb their desires as exfoliated by imagination or fantasy. The control has never been wholly successful, for imagination, unless killed off entirely, will always vault over any limit set by reason, rules, or anything else man can invent. Some of the most potent controls are themselves the result of imagination, e.g., the fear of punishment by ghostly monitors.

Education is one of the institutionalized efforts to make desires, real and imaginary, conform to what is permitted. It reinforces the legal system, the mores of the community, and the validity of the system as a whole. It rewards loyalty to the system of which it is a part. It tries to transmute the commands of the group into the desires of the young and to infect them above all with a desire to be approved by the group. It is through education that science is used to control the imagination of the young and thus indirectly to bring to bear the control of reality on the reasonings of the pupil.

These are the negative aspects of control. But there is a positive control of the imagination, exerted by images. Myths and art have been major sources of such images; they portray the desire system of the group. In our own time the machinery for creating and purveying images is not limited to works of art or myths. The mass media produce images wholesale on every aspect of life, and they do so with an impact that is almost irresistible. It is not for nothing that political figures regard their images as of more importance than their platforms and their appearance as more potent than their principles.

Here we stumble across the peculiar function of the school. Although it is charged with preserving the values or desire systems of the group, it is also entrusted with the responsibility of inducting the young into the cultural heritage of the group. Part of this heritage are the systems of thought and feeling that have crystallized out of centuries of critical reflection about what is real, true, good, and beautiful. In this heritage are not only the fruits of previous thought but also the tools for appraising these fruits; the heritage is revolutionary as well as conservationist. If this were not so, it would be difficult to see how our civilization could progress, in any useful meaning of that term. On the one hand, if the controls of desire and imagination were merely negative, the variation needed for evolution would not be tolerated. On the other hand, if our civilization has progressed and not merely changed, it must be because the variations "selected" for survival were chosen because of some principle or norm or ideal.

In our own civilization two great human contrivances have constituted the cultural heritage. One — that of science — controls (positively and negatively) our thinking about actuality, especially as regards our understanding the way of things. The other shapes our valuings, prizings, desirings, judgings. This is the system of the humanities — history, literature, the other fine arts, philosophy, and theology. Both parts of the tradition are conservative and critical — conservative in that they keep alive the norms of the past and their exemplars, critical in that they conserve only what seems to a given epoch to be the most signifi-

cant of these products. The induction of the young into these living traditions is a way of introducing them into enlightened
cherishing. However, this essay will concentrate more on the
humanities and the arts than on the scientific tradition. And I
would justify this emphasis on the following grounds.

First, there is no real controversy about the importance of
science and the authority for what constitutes "good" science.
The schools can and do adopt the criterion of the learned and
wise in science, i.e., the scientists whose names can be found in
the official directories of the learned societies. There is no such
consensus on the importance of the humanities, especially when
it comes to a legitimate authority for what constitutes "good"
choosing and "good" feeling. More will be said about the problem of authority.

The second reason is that the control of desires, especially the
realm of desire expanded by imagination, by the standard methods — social pressure and knowledge — has not proved effective
in value education. It may be wise, therefore, to look more closely
into the relations among imagination, feeling, valuing, and
choosing. What can education do with these processes? Can they
be ordered in a rationally defensible way, i.e., without being
arbitrarily imposed on the young?

A third reason, perhaps a variant of the first, has already been
mentioned: imagination has rarely been the prime target of
schoolwork. The cultivation of the logical and scientific powers
has been the prime target, and while this has been and must continue to be a salutary emphasis, it tends to inhibit the development of imagination.

It is perhaps not wholly a semantic accident that in our own
times "imaginative" and "beautiful" have become good words.
To be sure, the use of these terms is so indiscriminate that they
convey little more than general approbation. Nevertheless, that
the young have accepted them as honorific terms indicates how
both imagination and beauty, the twin attributes of the aesthetic

dimension of life, have suffered in contemporary life. Let us note also that in the current usage "beautiful" means not only what is aesthetically pleasing but more often what is thought to be morally good and metaphysically true. This is a return to the identity of the true, good, and beautiful, which Plato complained that art had failed to maintain. Although this identity is debatable and certainly most difficult to demonstrate, the possibility of aesthetic education contributing anything important to value education does presuppose, if not a unity, then certainly important areas of commonality. These we must now explore.

II

The Aesthetic Image

W HATEVER is valued by anyone has grown out of that person's desires for sensory gratification, love, power, self-esteem, glory, self-realization, and self-integration. Any list of generic drives will do. Our human nature is grounded in our animal nature. Any object that is perceived as having a positive connection with such desires or interests will serve as a stand-in for the actual experience. For example, the image of a large, powerful automobile will create in somebody who is fond of large, powerful cars the wish to possess one like it. Most advertising appeals to people's desires in this way; it shows them an image of the things or activities they already desire. The image reminds them of what it is they crave.

This use of images puts little strain on the imagination of the customer. The image resembles what he wants or displays an idealized version of it; e.g., the girl advertising a new shampoo is beautiful, and one can be quite sure that the customer also wants to be beautiful. About the only strain on her imagination is to imagine herself looking like the girl in the advertisement. Indeed, most large-scale advertising says something like this: "Imagine yourself owning this, being this, doing that."

Madison Avenue's defense against the charge that advertising stimulates people to buy what they don't really need or want is that it is merely catering to what people already want. If they didn't want the new shampoo or the boat or the automobile, they wouldn't buy them, and advertising would be powerless to induce them to do so. To a large extent the latter part of the argument is valid. Less defensible is the claim that the advertised product is what the customer already wants. The customer may want and need an automobile, but he does not necessarily want an automobile that has expensive accoutrements that do nothing to improve its automotive properties. But Madison Avenue uses these accoutrements to stir the customer's imagination by equating them with status and the envy of one's peers. When such advertising results in the customer changing his value priorities so that adequate clothing, food, and education rank lower than his automobile, then Madison Avenue cannot plead that it is merely satisfying demands already in existence. It is in this stirring of the imagination that the great impact of advertising on value and value education consists.

Education also has a place for this straightforward appeal by means of the imagination to preferences already formed. We remind pupils of love of country by playing a patriotic song or reciting a patriotic poem. Or we show pictures of the Grand Canyon, the broad prairies, and the mountains that comprise the United States to remind the viewer of the vastness of the country and the pride of owning "a piece of it." The image used to remind us of values already formed can be a simple picture of the object or a symbol that does not in any way resemble it, e.g., the flag. I shall say little more about such uses of images in value education, not because they are unimportant but, rather, because these uses are fairly clear and need no further emphasis.

Some remarks have to be made with regard to the possible misuse of the aesthetic image to reinforce the conventional values. The advertising industry may do so to increase sales and profits, and totalitarian states may abuse the reminding-reinforcing symbol to maintain social and political control. But if the school in the American culture has a liberating, progressive role as well as a conservative one, then it has to be just as careful in deciding what it will conserve by means of images as what it will conserve through knowledge. Much depends on our conception of the role of the school, and the one that I shall defend is that the primary function of the school is not the direct preservation or overthrow of any political or economic system but, rather, the development of the intellectual and evaluational powers of the individual. In doing so, the school uses the cultural heritage that the critical tradition has conserved, but part of the tradition is the cultivated imagination. From this imaginative power emerge the variations which form the matrix of progress.

But there is another sort of image and another use of images which I shall call a value import image or an aesthetic image. Perhaps we can best get at this kind of image by examining such everyday judgments as "The sky is threatening," "That man has a dishonest face," "The dog looks sick." To support these judgments and countless others like them, we use as evidence the appearance of something, the sky, the face, the dog. What we mean ordinarily, if pushed to explain our language, is something like this: Great storms can be dangerous, and the appearance of the sky prior to storms is dark, cloudy, and agitated, or it may have an eerie yellowish tinge. When the sky has this appearance, it looks as if it were warning us of impending danger; it therefore looks threatening.

Similarly, when we say that a man's face is dishonest, we probably have in mind a composite facial pattern associated with dishonest characters in plays and with such dishonest characters as we have encountered. But I would say that the dishonesty pattern is more likely to have been formed by the stereotypes of popular art than by experience with real thieves or embezzlers. Empirical tests rarely reveal criminal types of facial configurations. Why these patterns were chosen by the artists to stereotype in the first place, we do not know, but the deviousness of the thief is hardly congruent with "straight" lines or "straightforward" looks in the eye. Neither would it do to make the thief stand "upright" or let him stride in a direct route from one place to another. Moral crookedness displays itself in visual crookedness. To portray stealthiness in musical form, one would not employ tuneful melodies or vigorous rhythms.

The dramatist or the actor has to register character traits in large strokes or the audience will not see them; hence there is a premium on highly simplified and exaggerated expressions of fear, anger, surprise, and the other standard emotions. It is in this sense that the popular arts, especially, are our teachers of emotional expression. In real life we are nowhere so sure about the emotions people around us are experiencing; aside from reflex reactions to seeing a snake or dodging a missile, their responses are controlled and often concealed. It is only when we are asked to objectify our emotions — as in a play or story — that we realize how much we depend on the stereotypes employed by the popular arts. The musical portrait of the standard emotions in any given period is provided by popular music, and popular fiction is our resource for the standard images of emotional response in situations ranging from husbands announcing that they are having illicit affairs to mothers and daughters trying to "understand" each other.[1]

The image of sickness is conveyed by the drooping position of the dog's head and tail, the limpness of the body, unusual slowness of movement — all characteristic of weakness.

We tend to forget how many of our judgments about the characters of things and persons are based on the "looks" and

[1] One of the systematic attempts to trace the value schema of a period through its popular arts is Donald Arnstine's doctoral dissertation, "The Aesthetic Dimension of Value Education," at the University of Illinois, 1960. Currently Miss Myung Hee Han is doing a somewhat similar analysis in terms of Korean culture.

"sounds" of things, i.e., their appearances. That is why, among other factors, appearances are so important in first impressions. We do not consort with most people often enough for them to learn of our invisible virtues, so their judgment tends to be based on appearances. Many a lovely character has never been discovered simply because the first meeting did not invite further exploration. Conversely, many a man has made his way further than his talents warranted simply because the image he offered the world was attractive or reassuring as to strength and ability.

We are all familiar with the short man who feels that he must overcompensate for an unfavorable image by excessive energy and aggressiveness. In these days, when all disadvantaged groups are charging discrimination, none has a better right to complain than those whom nature has disfavored aesthetically. They are discriminated against doubly: first by a lack of seductiveness — which is in itself no mean source of power — and second because their appearance may well give a falsely unfavorable impression of their ability and character. One is reluctant to urge legislation to prevent discrimination in this sphere, but if legislation here promises little in the way of remedy, one can also see why legislation has such a hard time remedying other forms of discrimination that are based on aesthetic stereotypes, e.g., the black and the female images. Nothing fixes a stereotype so firmly as an aesthetic image, for the image gives the illusion that it *is* the reality — that blackness is per se bad, inferior, that shortness in a man is inferiority on legs, so to speak. As we shall have many occasions to comment, reason cannot break down prejudices that the popular arts reinforce; only sensitivity to more serious art can counter the persuasive effects of popular art stereotypes.

The power of the aesthetic image to influence desire, choice, and judgment lies in the value import it suggests or portrays. However, unlike the sort of image which serves as a reminder of some specific feeling, the aesthetic image does not remind us of this or that duty, this or that preference, this or that need.

Rather, the image looks or sounds like some emotional quality, some feeling tone, idea, or other experiential complex.[2]

Marlowe in *Faustus* says:

> O, thou art fairer than the evening air
> Clad in the beauty of a thousand stars;

This image is not that of the face or figure of any particular "thou"; how could it be? It is an image of fairness, not of a person. Yet could any image be more vivid and definite than this one is?

Shakespeare has Richard II say:

> Within the hollow crown
> That rounds the mortal temples of a king
> Keeps Death his court: and there the antic sits
> Scoffing his state and grinning at his pomp:

This is a wry commentary on the pride of power, but its effectiveness depends on a thousand associations we have formed among death, king, crown, court, pomp, jesters, and grins. Not one association for each word, but literally a thousand bits and pieces of feeling and imagery have coalesced in clusters and folds that these lines of poetry now reinstate.

A reading of John Livingston Lowes's studies of the ingredients of Coleridge's imagery or Grover Smith's account of the associations, allusions, and references in T. S. Eliot's works will indicate the enormous complexity out of which emerge what seem to be simple images.

Arts other than poetry work in analogous ways. Every motion in a melody is like a trace of a human emotion, rising, falling, blending, getting into and falling out of relation with other motions. It has been said that the rhythms of the body, nature, and the seasons are the roots which music taps for its effects: ". . . if feeling is a culmination of vital process, any articulated image of

[2] See, for example, Isabel C. Hungerland, "Iconic Signs and Expressiveness," *Journal of Aesthetics and Art Criticism* 3, nos. 11-12 (n.d.): 15-21.

it must have the semblance of that vital process rising from deep, general organic activities to intense and concerted acts, such as we perceive directly in their psychical phases as impacts or felt actions. Every artistic form reflects the dynamism that is constantly building up the life of feeling."[3] But every work of art that has a rhythm of any sort also taps the same roots. Inhaling, exhaling, sudden bursts of energy, conflicts and resolutions, seeding and budding, endless variations of species characteristics — all of these are the ultimate building blocks of both the aesthetic image and the life processes. They are more fundamental operations than working, falling in love, winning a game, losing a wife, or building a bridge, in the same sense that molecules and their interactions are more fundamental than the objects and events which they constitute and explain.

It is not unreasonable to suppose that living processes leave their traces in consciousness and perhaps in the subconsciousness. Every conflict, with its passions, terrors, and triumphs, every yearning and frustration, one might suppose, had its counterpart in the life of feeling, but in time the links between events and their corresponding feelings weakened, and instead of clear one-to-one correspondences a pool of feeling tones came to represent a pool of experiences of many kinds. Thus each event and feeling could arouse not one but many associations. Accordingly, the words "fairer than the evening air" strike us as neither wholly familiar nor wholly strange. Stars, evening air, and, one might add, moonlight are intimately associated in the minds of men with splendor, wonder, and mystery. That stars and moon are like lanterns or other means of illumination to dispel the terror of night is a very old and familiar figure of speech. Deep, dark night is for foul deeds and violence; starry heavens are for gentle deeds and romance.

In some such fashion, it would seem, are the multilayered

[3] Susanne K. Langer, *Mind: An Essay on Human Feeling* (Baltimore: Johns Hopkins Press, 1967), 1: 199.

meanings formed, which make it possible for works of art to convey meaning through images. The point to be made is that the same process of storage, transformation, retrieval, and creation occurs in both the artist and the beholder. The beholder may lack the genius to create the image or, as Benedetto Croce would say, to form an individual intuition of it, but the depth and scope of his imagic associations will determine the scope and depth of the beholder's response. Responses can be complex or simple, rich or impoverished, stereotyped or vividly original; one cannot predict what they will be. If we could predict the response, we would not be dealing with art or with aesthetic experience; we would be doing empirical psychology. Perhaps one day psychology will be able to predict the responses to all possible stimuli. On that day there will be little room for imagination, and the psychologists will have cured us of it. That would give us a more orderly and, no doubt, more efficient world, but it would no longer be recognized as human by humans, if, as was argued above, to be human is to imagine what might be and ought to be. For one of the things imagination might concoct is the possibility that the laws which would enable psychologists to predict our responses would themselves be outwitted.

DIMENSIONS OF AESTHETIC EXPERIENCE

Experience with images that have value import we shall call aesthetic experience, and the peculiar sort of images involved in the aesthetic transaction can be called aesthetic images or objects. The aesthetic experience is a compound of imagination and perception, and although the phenomenon is common enough in everyday life, we tend to become explicitly aware of it only when we are confronted with works of art. Although a work of art is designed to trigger our imaginative perception, any object whatever can under appropriate circumstances be perceived aesthetically; that is, its appearance may be attended to as conveying some intimation of value. Aesthetic experience, although it is not disconnected from our intellectual life and our practical endeavors, has some features which make it distinctive.[4]

Without trying to give a formal definition of aesthetic object, the work of art, the aesthetic experience, or even the aesthetic image, one may point out several characteristics that all of these terms share and that some other types of experience do not.

The Sensory Dimension

The aesthetic object, whether natural, e.g., a mountain or forest, or a work of art in any medium, is an image or a cluster of images. In paintings the images are visual; in poetry the words are supposed to conjure up images; in drama the actors create visual images; in music the images are tonal; in the dance they are visual and musical. In aesthetic experience we deal not with abstract ideas or theories but, rather, with particular images — a particular poem, drama, story, etc. Hence aesthetic experience is in the first instance perceptual.[5]

However, in aesthetic perception the object has to be perceived as a particular individual entity and in its entirety. This is important for education, because very few of the activities in the classroom — as in life — make a point of perceiving the object in its entirety. In scientific observation we perceive carefully, but only those features of an object that are relevant to the under-

[4] There is general agreement that aesthetic experience has some unique properties; the agreement ends when it comes to the properties that are unique — hence the difficulty (some would say impossibility) of defining aesthetic experience or works of art. See Morris Weitz's "The Role of Theory in Aesthetics," *Journal of Aesthetics and Art Criticism* 15 (1956): 27-35, and Maurice Mandelbaum's comments on it in "Family Resemblances and Generalizations Concerning the Arts," *American Philosophical Quarterly* 11 (1965): 219-228.

[5] Some argue that this is too sweeping a characterization. They would hold that the aesthetic object need not be a sensory image, e.g., the aesthetic aspect of a mathematical formulation or the elegance of a theory. For aesthetic education this debatable reservation is not crucial.

standing of theory. For example, we ask the class to observe carefully what happens when an ignited splint is inserted in a tube filled with oxygen and in one filled with carbon dioxide, but we do not ask the pupils to perceive the size, shape, or color of the splint. The oxygen as such is not perceptible at all.

As an example of translating an idea into a particular image, consider the following:

> An aged man is but a paltry thing,
> A tattered coat upon a stick, unless
> Soul clap its hands and sing, and louder sing
> For every tatter in its mortal dress.[6]

To be sure, these are words about ideas of old age, and if we did not know the English language, we could not manage the poem at all, save perhaps to sense its rhythm and sound patterns. But if we do know the English language, and if our store of meanings and value import images is adequate, then these words create an image of these ideas. An *aged* man is not equivalent to an old man; it connotes a man worn down by age: in this line "aged" does not convey the idea of improving with age. We are now presented with an image of a scarecrow, nothing inside and nothing much outside except the remnants of a garment. But it is an idea that is being made perceptible in an image; it is not the picture of an old man. An old man as a body is a paltry thing unless "soul clap its hands and sing." The image for the redemptive power of the soul (a very abstract idea) is clapping and singing in praise and exaltation of something. The point I am trying to make is that although there is no picture of an old man, the words of the poem create visually vivid images of old age. They may be images of ideas, but they are also images of feelings and feelings about ideas.

The sensory properties of the aesthetic image are essential properties and to change them changes the object. Color photog-

[6] William Butler Yeats, "Sailing to Byzantium," *Collected Poems* (New York: Macmillan, 1928).

raphy cannot be equated with black and white; the sensory properties of marble cannot be found in sculpture made of welded auto fenders. As we shall see, the habit of apprehending the sensory properties of objects in their fullness and richness is the first step in aesthetic education.

The Formal Properties

The aesthetic image is to be perceived by the senses, even when the image is of an idea, as of old age or an attitude toward old age. In the lines quoted from Yeats's poem there is a mixture of contempt for old age and perhaps a trace of resentment against losing the bodily vigor of youth. It takes a lot of soul clapping its hands and singing to make up for the loss. Yet the image of a tattered coat upon a stick, while saying nothing directly about old age, carries a great freight of feelings, many of which we cannot name, let alone explain.

How does the poem get its power? Why does it hold our attention in a way that a dozen real old men cannot? One answer is form. Technically, we call the arrangement of the words and the corresponding images the *form* of the poem, but the term covers many aspects of the aesthetic image. First of all, it means design or composition. For example, the meter and rhyme create sound patterns which are not those of prose or ordinary speech. The movement of ordinary speech has not been harnessed, measured, and matched. The poet has made an effort to arrange these sound patterns, and after reading a line or two, we fall into its rhythm and adjust our expectations. Why certain patterns please us I do not know. Perhaps because certain designs are present everywhere in nature, and when we find them clarified and made obvious by the artist, we respond to them with interest and pleasure, as if we were meeting the children of parents we knew a long time ago.

So it is with the piece of music or the carefully constructed drama or painting. The artist by selection throws into strong relief rhythms, variations of a theme, balances, and contrasts. He weaves a great variety into a unity, so that it seems as if nothing in it could have been omitted without destroying the whole work. Real life is not that orderly; the sounds of the street are not ordered as in a musical composition. There are perhaps many fine scenes in the world around us, but it takes the artist's eye to detect their pictorial possibilities.

Furthermore, the order imposed by the artist on his materials betrays the human mind at work. When we come across a piece of driftwood with an interesting shape, we are apt to say that it looks as if someone had carved it that way, as if wind and water could not have arrived at that form mindlessly. Yet natural things betray an even deeper penetration of order. The work of art exhausts its order on the surface; beneath the paint there is meaningless canvas so far as art is concerned. But in every molecule and atom of the canvas there is pattern and order; whether it carries *human* import, however, is another matter, and that is why one may hesitate to speak of nature as the Great Artist.

We expend much money and care to extirpate from our lawns the dandelions that flourish there every spring. As far as the quality of sensory experience is concerned, there is much to be said for the vivid colors of the dandelion flower, and its leaves are more interesting than the leaves of grass for which we sacrifice them. Yet should some suburban householder plant dandelions in carefully contrived patterns on his lawn, we would regard them with interest and probably with admiration. Dandelions growing at random on a lawn are not in themselves ugly, but letting them grow creates the image of a careless householder indifferent to the sensibilities of his neighbors. But carefully cultivated dandelions, i.e., given aesthetic form, are a different story. They are witness to care and concern for appearance; they constitute an appropriate expression of suburban virtue.

Sensory images or materials arranged for the greatest impact on perception constitute the formal properties of art. Form provides the unity in variety that captures and retains our interest, and to the degree that life fails to provide such unity, art is valued all the more for doing so.

A carpet or wallpaper with an intricately organized design contributes the order so dear to us even though it may have no profound significance, as has a poem on old age. The contrived bed of dandelions can delight the eye even though no great human issues revolve around it. Picasso's *Guernica,* while it, too, is a unified complex of sensory images, stirs a different sort of interest. It brings together in one vivid — almost overwhelming — impression a vast complexity of feeling and ideas about the violence and brutality of war. Art which touches the great human themes — love, conflict, death, redemption — is sometimes called "great" art, and it is to this sort of art that people have reference when they think of value education through art. In a later section I shall have more to say about the principles of organization that contribute the form which produces unity in variety in a work of art. For the moment I would like to return to the question of why certain formal structures capture our attention and hold our interest.

John Dewey in *Art as Experience*[7] made the now famous distinction between experiences and *an* experience. Experience as such is a flow of awareness of varying content and quality. The stream-of-consciousness technique used by Joyce, Proust, and others simulates the endless odd lots of baggage that make up our lives, much as a moving belt conveying all sorts of trunks, bags, and cases makes up the lives of customs inspectors. To make *an* experience out of this flow, says Dewey, we must select events that are cumulative in their impact. The second phase augments and builds on the first, the third on the first and second, and so on. *An* experience has a beginning, a development, a climax, and

[7] (New York: G. P. Putnam's Sons, 1958; first published 1934).

a resolution that rounds it off, thus making it stand out.[8] The original is now seen in the light of what has happened subsequently. *An* experience, we may say, is characterized by a quality that pervades it and thereby distinguishes it from other experiences. But the pervasive quality is vivid, somewhat in the way that flavor becomes vivid in concentrates.

Dewey says many things about the conditions for having *an* experience, and it is not at all clear that they are consistent with each other.[9] To my mind, however — although I would not want to attribute this view to Dewey — what makes experience "an experience" is dramatic structure. Experience as such does not ordinarily have dramatic quality. An insignificant life is precisely one in which no dramatic unity can be discerned. It takes a novelist to imbue ordinary people's lives with drama. It takes a historian to discern the drama in social movements, and only long after the events have occurred, for it takes time to sort out what had been crucial to the plot and what had been only incidental. While we are living through events, we do not know what will turn out to be significant.

That dramatic form is a key to interest and significance is easily illustrated. When we recount an episode that we think of as significant, we give it dramatic form — suspense as to the outcome, some element of danger, some sense of climax, and, if possible, an unexpected ending. To make it interesting, we omit certain details and emphasize others; poor story tellers do just the opposite and often end up by forgetting what the point of the story was. There is a latent natural capacity for the dramatic in all of us.

This is illustrated further by the reaction of the public to such events as the assassinations of the Kennedys and Martin Luther

[8] *Ibid.,* p. 35.
[9] See, for example, C. M. Smith, "The Aesthetics of John Dewey and Aesthetic Education," *Educational Theory* 21, no. 2 (Spring 1971), and D. W. Gotshalk, "On Dewey's Aesthetics," *Journal of Aesthetics and Art Criticism* 30, no. 1 (Fall 1964).

King. Despite the preponderance of evidence to the contrary, many people believe that these assassinations were the results of deep and far-flung conspiracies. Why? Because they cannot believe that great effects could result from insignificant causes. It is hard to believe that important public figures can die as a result of simple accidents, or the deranged impulses of very insignificant people, or even sheer miscalculation. In other words, the literal truth, which is likely to be drab and formless as life itself can be, is hard to live with. The literal truth is a confusing mélange of happenings, a tale seemingly told by an idiot and tolerable only to idiots, whose minds are also confused, or to sages, who can see in the confusion a drama that is being played out. For most of us — neither idiots nor sages — truth must be converted into a plausible fiction, that is, given dramatic form so that it makes sense. And so we conjure up conspiracies to render assassinations, wars, and the doings of legislators credible. Our criteria for credibility are, more often than not, aesthetic.

Is the dramatizing of experience a piece of fakery? Does it spawn mischievous illusion? Is it a revelation of or an escape from reality? This is the theme of much theorizing about the role of art in life. We do not have to settle this issue here. It may be enough to note that for human beings, significance means human import, and what has such import if not events that create and dissolve conflict and danger? Hence we speak of the human drama with its heroes and villains, and this drama is part of a cosmic drama also replete with heroes and villains. If all of experience is a drama, then the subordinate little episodes may have a part in the total drama, and our search for dramatic form takes on a cosmic or metaphysical grandeur. Conversely, if our own little dramas have no connection with a larger drama, then they are either illusions or they are not connected with each other in any essential way. Life may have no overall significance yet be made up of significant episodes, like jewels on a string rather than as parts of a tiara. We can assert the latter possibility even if we are unsure of the former, and this is why each segment of experience that has aesthetic or dramatic form can be cherished for its own sake. Its vividness, its *inherent* unity, gives it a self-contained value that requires no further justification. We say that it has intrinsic value; it is *an* experience. The search for significance, therefore, goes through the aesthetic route as well as the scientific one. A form of life that has dramatic structure does not guarantee its ultimate goodness for others or even for oneself. Some dramas are tragedies, and some turn out to be obscene comedies, but it is human to prefer that risk to the safety of insignificance. The aesthetically satisfying experience is the opposite of the drab, meaningless, formless, pointless passage of time.

I am aware that some aestheticians, and perhaps all of them, would balk at equating aesthetic form with dramatic structure, and I would concede that some patterns of rhythm, of balance and contrast, theme and variation, do not have a plot, suspense, and climax. Purely decorative patterns in wallpapers, carpets, and architectural borders can be interesting despite their lack of dynamics, and yet I find myself wondering what in these "formal" forms commands our attention and interest.

There must be some tension to command attention, some opposition and resolution to avoid sheer monotony and triviality. But tensions and resolution, however stylized and formalized they may be, are dramatic. Even the uniform pattern of a frieze or the stylized grape patterns on the capital of a column are a startling contrast to the rash distribution of forms in nature and ordinary life. How often can this pattern be repeated without distortion and variation? This question itself sets up a tension.

Sensitivity to aesthetic form is at the heart of aesthetic experience and aesthetic education. Another way of saying this is to say that sensitivity to the dramatic structure of aesthetic images is what differentiates an aesthetically developed person from one who is not. The stereotyped drama of ordinary life can be sensed without special cultivation. An automobile accident, a murder, or a diplomatic crisis we can apprehend and respond to without special training. The import of these events is so obvious and pressing that it would be impossible not to be interested in them. Nor does it take cultivation to respond to the mystery story, the soap opera, the popular fiction that deliberately dramatizes extraordinary episodes of life. But aesthetic experience can go far beyond that. To experience life aesthetically is to sense the drama in every event of nature, in every moment of life, in the conflict of colors and shapes, sounds and rhythms. To go beyond stereotyped dramatics requires cultivation, as it does to go beyond stereotypes in any other type of experience.

The artist differs from the nonartist in being able to give form to sensory materials or to see form in them that most of us do not. This is disconcerting to the nonartist because for him, dramatic form to be discernible has to be writ large in plots and conspiracies, in great misfortunes and disasters. Artists find dramatic form everywhere. Aesthetic insensitivity is a clue to our unhappiness with life. For inability to sense subtle significance makes our lives drab, routinized, and boring. It renders us vulnerable to drugs and other bizarre stimulations in search for proof that we are alive and not existential zeros. The need for such proof is a sign of desperation, what Sören Kierkegaard called existential despair.

Dramatic form may not be the equivalent of moral or religious or metaphysical significance, but it is the first intimation of it. God in the creation first gave the formless void form, and it was the dramatic form of a story which would in time disclose the human drama, its beginning, fall, and redemption. Subsequent disclosures of science make the story less dramatic and argue that it is no more than a plausible fiction. But there is a limit to dedramatization. When science brings us to the point where we cannot dramatize the cosmic story at all, it will have become dehumanized and we with it. Human life will indeed have become a tale told by an idiot for the delectation of idiots only.

The aesthetic mode of experience in bringing us these episodic gems of life exploits both our persistent craving for the cosmic drama and our skepticism about there being one. Not being sure there is a cosmic drama that makes all of life intelligible and tolerable, we seize on fragments of life the vividness and significance of which we cannot doubt, and we cherish them for what they are, not for what might lie beyond or beneath them. Yet craving for drama dies hard, and so plausible fictions will be with us as long as we remain human.

Expressiveness of the Aesthetic Image

So much for the first two dimensions of the aesthetic experience or the response to the aesthetic image — the sensory and the formal. Sensory materials formed into an image may carry more or less value import, but some import it must carry. The design on the carpet, the ordering of sounds into simple rhymes and rhythms may not carry the significance of human dramas. Nevertheless, they are never merely literal renderings of the actual world. The repeated pattern in a carpet is not a copy of something in nature, even though it may be the abstract of a flower and therewith derived from a natural form. To stylize the flower into a simple shape repeated again and again is the artist's judgment about what is characteristic of the flower. He has taken what to him is the most important aspect of the flower and left out everything else. As for the repetition of the flower pattern, does it not celebrate a victory over nature to be able to arrange such a profusion of delightful patterns according to our desires? Nature is not always so accommodating.

The value import of an aesthetic image may be called its expressiveness. The expressiveness of the aesthetic image has two salient characteristics. One is that it is metaphorical and the other is that it is presentational; it is in one sense indirect and in another sense very direct.

When a painting such as Grant Wood's *American Gothic* is said to express something about the American character or the midwestern American rural character, what do we mean? Strictly or literally speaking, faces and figures have no such character traits as sternness, moral rigidity, and uprightness, traits which the Grant Wood figures are supposed to express. Only persons and their tendencies toward certain types of behavior can be said to have such traits. For example, if the persons depicted by Wood consistently condemned drinking, dancing, undue levity in children, and the like, we could properly attribute to them the character of moral rigidity or something called puritanical morality. But lines and colored patterns cannot be said to have moral character. If they do express character traits, it must be indirectly: if moral rigidity were to be translated into facial patterns, it would look something like these faces do.

This, however, is a figure of speech. Similarly, if we say that Beethoven's Fifth opens with a menacing theme, we mean that if menace could be translated into tonal patterns, it would sound like the opening bars of Beethoven's Fifth. Thus facial features, bodily postures, and gestures are said to be expressive in the drama and in the dance, yet if they say anything it is in a figure of speech. Literally, they make no sense. Sometimes the word "synaesthesia" is used to denote the mixing up of the sensory modalities, as when we say that something smells green or that something has a dark brown taste, or when we sometimes wish that the coffee would taste as it smells. In the aesthetic image, however, sensory image and feelings are combined. Cheerfulness, excitement, tension, strictly speaking, are qualities of human experience, and when visual or auditory shapes are said to have these qualities, we are talking in metaphors. I say metaphors because the aesthetic image does not say "I am *like* something which I have no business being literally," but rather it announces itself as *being* that quality.

> In short, images have all the characteristics of symbols . . .
> we attend to them in their capacity of *meaning* things, being
> *images* of things — symbols whereby those things are con-
> ceived, remembered, considered, but not encountered.
>
> The best guarantee of their essentially symbolic function is
> their tendency to become metaphorical. They are not only
> capable of connoting the things from which our sense-experi-
> ence originally derived them, and perhaps, by the law of
> association, the context in which they were derived (as the
> sight of a bell may cause one to think of "ding-dong" and
> also of dinner), but they also have an inalienable tendency to
> "mean" things that have only a logical analogy to their pri-
> mary meanings. The image of a rose symbolizes feminine
> beauty so readily that it is actually harder to associate roses
> with vegetables than with girls. Fire is a natural symbol of
> life and passion, though it is the one element in which noth-
> ing can actually live.[10]

I want to concentrate for the moment on the differences among the sight of a bell symbolizing dinner or "ding-dong," the rose symbolizing feminine beauty, and fire symbolizing life and pas-sion. The sight of the bell, as Langer notes, reminds us of the sound and the dinner because of previous association. The sight, the sound, and the dinner have been experienced together so frequently that one reminds us of the others.

A rose does not remind us of feminine beauty simply because we have experienced the two together frequently — I am not at all sure that we have — but rather because the artists and poets have asserted a fundamental similarity or affinity between them. In this they are aided by the fact that roses are themselves regarded as beautiful to sight, and, like beautiful women (at least in west-ern culture), they have an exotic fragrance. Furthermore, the velvety texture of rose petals is like the texture of a beautiful

[10] Susanne K. Langer, *Philosophy in a New Key* (New York: New American Library, 1948), p. 117.

woman's skin. Finally, the beauty of the rose, like that of women, is often protected by thorny barriers.

The relation of fire to passion is more subtle. There is little perceptual resemblance between the phenomena of life, fire, and passion. However, certain properties of fire are essential to life and passion, e.g., heat and restless energy that consumes and transforms but which nevertheless gives light and warmth. We speak of the spark of life and the coldness of death; the heat of the sun and its light are essential to life. Hence fire is a natural image of life and passion.

No doubt these natural analogies are at the root of our basic imagery, the most basic perhaps being the analogy between living human beings and the animals and plants that surround them. Mythology endows animals with human characteristics and vice versa. Spirits inhabit trees, rivers, and rocks; witness the burning bush and the water-giving rock in the Moses story. Science and common sense may have freed our thinking from this primordial anthropomorphism, this mixing up of human and nonhuman, animate and inanimate objects, but the stock of imagery serving the race has never rid itself of this confusion; art would be impossible without it.

As children grow up, the imagery of stories is supplemented by their own imaginative combinations (for example, when a five-year-old speaks of eraser rubbings as mistake dust or of dreams as movies in the air). But challenging these images are the literal descriptions of the actual world. In our culture, it is fair to say, the imaginative life loses out to the reality principle, especially as practical needs become more urgent. In real life money, not fairy godmothers, supplies candy and ice cream; the real villain is the doctor who wields a needle, not a grotesque witch brandishing a magic wand. As literalness takes over, communion with nature atrophies, for it is only in the world of imagination that men and beasts are intermingled as kindred spirits. When this innocence is lost, nature becomes the domain of science, where fact, not drama, has the last word.

As literalness pervades our lives, more and more of the world becomes nonexpressive. Or, more correctly, more and more items in the world are perceived as signposts reminding us of things associated with them casually or causally. The cloudy sky is seen as a sign of rain and getting wet, or it is associated with memories of events associated with cloudy skies, some important, some trivial. Life becomes prosaic, losing its vividness and its dramatic quality. It is no longer intrinsically interesting, as D. W. Gotshalk would say, to perception. We do not linger over signposts but hurry on to places they designate.

The practical, scientific attitudes, so necessary and important to life, render us less sensitive to metaphor. We no longer accept the structural affinity between fire and passion, the blue sky and a smiling child. Ritual and myth are put away as childish things, so that when significant events do occur, we celebrate them clumsily, almost with embarrassment. Birth, wedding, and death are marked by remnants of ancient rituals the impact of which has been diluted because we are so afraid that we shall fool ourselves into thinking that they somehow have power to evoke the real thing. Still another way of putting the point is to say that the loss of sensitivity to metaphorical perception shrinks the domain of value experience. Science gives us laws describing phenomena, and technology provides us with ways of controlling these phenomena through our scientific knowledge about them. But the significance of things and events for human valuation is given neither by science nor by technology.

If this sounds trite and on the rhetorical side, consider the age-old question about why men spend their lives in hard work long after their physiological needs are satisfied. To understand this peculiar phenomenon, we must capture the metaphor which guides such men's lives. There are many such metaphors. "I am the captain of my soul" is one; the tale of the industrious ant and the lazy grasshopper is another. The image of the great father, provider, and controller is another. Power is good because it is godlike, and money is power. When we ask the question "What am I *really*, what is my identity?," we are really asking "What metaphor applies to me?" We are what we are, but no further light is thrown on our question until we ask what we are *like*, so that we can plausibly fuse ourselves with that with which we have an important affinity. This affinity is the cue to our identity. What metaphor will express me? With what image can I feel at one? Is not this the question being asked, for example, by the sincere advocate of women's liberation? She rejects the metaphors of a rose, a violet, a fertility goddess, a mantrap, a servant of the lord and master. But what new metaphor is to replace these? She does not know and we do not know; art has not yet conjured it up.

The artist is the source of the original, the unusual, the fresh, the apt metaphor. Although he draws on the memory bank of the race, he does not simply repeat what he finds there. Who, without the aid of the poet, would find such metaphors as Shakespeare's "We are such stuff / As dreams are made on, and our little life / Is rounded with a sleep," or Shelley's "Bright reason will mock thee / Like the sun from a wintry sky," or Keats's "The moving waters at their priestlike task / Of pure ablution round earth's human shores." Again we must not forget that metaphors are found in all artistic media and are not confined to the linguistic ones. To perceive a tonal pattern as a human feeling or to see *American Gothic* as puritanical character is to perceive a metaphor.

Accordingly, in aesthetic education we are speaking about the cultivation of the pupil's receptivity to expressiveness via metaphor. This expressiveness is achieved by giving form to a sensory content, creating a surface on which meaning and value import are presented directly for imaginative perception. If works of art have any "message" — and many a formalist denies that they do — it is because there are similarities between all sorts of objects and ideas. Through these resemblances we discover something important about what to love and what to hate, what to cherish and what to disdain. We learn something about ourselves when we imagine what a rock would feel if it had a mind and soul.

The role of art in aesthetic education is twofold. One is to objectify for perception those metaphors which the imagination of the artist creates. These help the pupil to objectify his own feelings and values. In doing so they expand his value domain, for they reveal life possibilities not available through direct experience. The second role of art is to purify the pupil's imagic store and thereby to make him more conscious of and less satisfied with the stereotyped image and the worn-out metaphor. In this sense it makes pupils more discriminating both about art and about life itself.

AESTHETIC POVERTY AND CHARITY

The aesthetic image is the distinctive unit of aesthetic experience. The artist creates it deliberately by giving dramatic structure to colors, shapes, textures, sounds, or gestures, depending on the medium of his art. The beholder perceives it imaginatively: not practically with a view to using it, not intellectually for the purpose of explaining it. Not all aesthetic images are produced by artists. Nature, the appearance of people, the sound of their speech — indeed, anything we can perceive — has some potentiality for being perceived aesthetically. That we do not respond aesthetically more often to our environment may be accounted for by at least two factors. One is the dominance of our need to perceive practically and intellectually. A motorist who becomes absorbed in the sensory qualities of a traffic light, and forgets to think of the lights as a set of commands, will not survive in a motor culture. Nor can we react to trees and rocks as if they harbored spirits, just as we cannot carry on modern agriculture by performing fertility rites. In becoming socialized, the child also learns to use his perception as a means to action and understanding rather than to exercise his imagination. Perception as a means to appreciation becomes peripheral and secondary.

The other factor lies in the environment itself. Not much of it is organized so as to delight the senses or stimulate imaginative perception. In town after town Main Street is lined with single-story rectangles put together with cinder blocks. Such buildings are so limited in their design that there is little anybody can do to make them "intrinsically interesting to perception." There are no surprises, no contrasts, no conflicts, no resolutions — in short, no life. They are containers: one glance is sufficient to identify their purpose and to dismiss their appearance; they do not warrant a second glance. People, especially women, do take the trouble to make their own appearance attractive. The new freedom in fashions presents an opportunity to make attire aesthetically interesting, and although much of this freedom has been squandered on the absurd and the bizarre, it still remains true that clothing for both sexes is more varied and individualized than it has been for at least a century.

One might wish that people devoted more care to the sound of their speech and its qualities of expression. Conversation is not only a lost art; it is no longer an art. There are discussions, debates, conferences, and chitchat but very little conversation. Conversation cannot be equated with communication or clarification or explanation. It is undertaken for the mutual delectation of the participants; it involves wit as well as good sense; it entails wanting to interest and perhaps entertain as well as to inform. A good conversation is a work of art in which the sensory qualities of speech, its form, and its expressiveness make talking "an experience." About the only interesting feature of ordinary discourse is slang, on which the young have a monopoly. For most people the monotony of everyday speech is relieved only by profanity and obscenity, and neither very original at that.

The aesthetic poverty of the environment is not necessarily the result of economic poverty; it is, rather, the result of disregard for the aesthetic sensibility of our fellow men. Our possessions are designed primarily for our own convenience and use; anything that does not obviously contribute to that use is dispensable. Only the rich are supposed to be able to indulge aesthetic considerations. But this is a misguided notion. And it is misguided because aesthetic quality is so often mistaken for symbols of status, wealth, and importance. Well-designed jewelry can be made from nonprecious metals, and attractive clothing is not confined to Parisian salons.

What is needed is not more money but more concern for the appearances of things as objects of aesthetic perception, and if we believe that clothing, speech, houses, and furniture, as well as lakes, mountains, and trees, can be expressive as well as useful, we shall not make the appearance of things the lowest item in our list of priorities. For there is such a thing as aesthetic charity or, if that is hard to achieve, then we should cultivate a sense of obligation to make that segment of the world under our control as interesting to perceive as possible. No matter how utilitarian an object is — a building or a food container — the moment we try to make it attractive, we begin to cherish it for itself as well as for its use. An ugly world is likely to be one in which people hate each other, fear each other, or are at best indifferent to each other. If aesthetic education is successful, it will reduce both the ugliness and the hate.

AESTHETIC APPRECIATION AND ENJOYMENT

It is appropriate to conclude this discussion of the aesthetic image with some reference to aesthetic appreciation or enjoyment. Indeed, the justification most frequently given for aesthetic education is that it enlarges the capacity for enjoyment. Yet in the description and analysis of the aesthetic image little has been said about enjoyment.

The reason for this omission is that although works of art and the beauties of nature are enjoyed, it is difficult to pin down in words the character of the enjoyment. To say that enjoyment means having pleasure does not remove the difficulty, because listening to music does not yield the same sort of pleasure as hearing over the radio that one has won the Irish Sweepstakes. Writers on the subject have used such terms as "aesthetic pleasure" or "aesthetic emotion" to differentiate the enjoyment derived from aesthetic experience from other kinds of pleasure. Unfortunately, giving the experience a name does not tell us what it is.

Clearly, the pleasure we are trying to identify is not the same as what we feel when we gratify an appetite for food, sex, money, or power. For in the latter cases we crave something in particular that will sate the craving. But in listening to music or viewing a painting we do not want to seize and hold the painting or the musicians. Nor does whatever desire for aesthetic experience we have wax to a climax and wane with fulfillment.

Aesthetic enjoyment is sensual, and yet not all sensual pleasures are aesthetic. Keeping the distinction clear is not easy because so much art is associated with and is rooted in nonaesthetic sensory pleasures. It is difficult to dissociate the anticipated or recollected pleasures of sexual gratification from the aesthetic pleasure derived from a painting of a female nude. How much of our aesthetic pleasure in a still life is an imagined delight of the palate? Yet if our satisfaction from aesthetic objects were no more than the intimations of bodily gratifications, then we would do better to pursue the real objects rather than aesthetic substitutes.

That aesthetic pleasure is not simply a thinned-out version of physiological gratification is proved by the fact that we do get pleasure from works of art in which there is no recognizable subject matter. There being no recognizable tables, chairs, fruits, or human figures in an abstract painting, the viewer attends to the formal properties of the work and their expressiveness. In music there is, as a rule, little to remind the listener of specific objects or events. The sensory, formal properties and their expressiveness are all there is.

In visual art, drama, and the dance, however, attention to the aesthetic dimensions requires some effort to achieve what Edward Bullough called "psychical distance," whereby one disinvolves oneself from the content of the work of art. The viewer must attend to the aesthetic qualities of which the real figures and objects are the bearers. Once the viewer has formed strong non-aesthetic associations with objects and figures, he cannot easily dissociate the delight in the objects themselves from the delight in the aesthetic properties. For this reason it is naive to believe that art cannot endanger morals. It can if the viewer is unable to perceive art objects aesthetically, and the untrained perceiver is likely to have this infirmity.

Why, then, do painters, dramatists, and choreographers use real objects if they are such an obstacle to aesthetic pleasure? One reason may be that real objects are the most direct vehicles of expressiveness. The grace, gentleness, and seductiveness of woman is a perennial theme of art; how can one express these abstract qualities better than by a representation of the human body? The trick is to see in the female nude painting or sculpture the essence of womanhood or some aspect of it and not to be overwhelmed by the illusion that this is a portrait of a particular woman whom one might possess. Much art, therefore, is properly erotic in that it expresses aesthetically certain life qualities which have to do with sex and love. To be sure, if the beholder of such works were not a humanly sexual creature, the painting or drama would lose its expressiveness for him altogether, but if the work is successful, the response is the delight that accompanies the insight into the nature of love, femininity, or tenderness. At most this is a fifth cousin to pornography, which incites the viewer to seek actual sexual gratification and nothing else.

This opinion is in accord with the view that the aesthetic object is the image of human passion expressed in a metaphor, and that there must be sufficient disengagement of the viewer from actuality that he can attend to the image of passion without becoming the vehicle of it. It is quite consistent, on this view, that we can "enjoy" a great tragedy on the stage. The tragedy allows us to understand the horror, which we cannot do if we are experiencing it directly. In this sense the enjoyment we derive from aesthetic experience is very much akin to the thrill of discovery, as Aristotle observed. This distinction between *having an emotion* and *contemplating the image of an emotion* is peculiarly important for aesthetic education.

In aesthetic education, however, one often hears the demand that the music or the play or the painting be moving, that it arouse some strong emotion and not necessarily an aesthetic emotion. In part this demand comes from the perennial problem of pedagogy, namely, catching and holding the attention of the pupil; and certainly that which moves us arouses our emotions, captures attention most effectively. But, as has already been noted, if to generate emotion is the goal, then exposure to art is not the most efficient way of doing it.

There is something more to the demand that experience with art be "moving." Parents and other adult authoritative figures want the young to be moved by art in order to become enthusiastic about the virtues of courage, honesty, patriotism, and prudence or, more accurately, about the behaviors that during a given period are taken as appropriate manifestations of the virtues. In this parents of all generations would agree with Plato that only those art works that celebrate the virtues of the group and their gods be taught in the schools. This means censorship, and this troubles parents who are against censorship where their own children are not concerned.[11]

Aesthetic education as training in imaginative perception avoids this Platonic dilemma. This approach tries to cultivate in the pupil a capacity for aesthetic pleasure and aesthetic emotion in general. The works that are used to accomplish this can vary over a very wide range, and while some may reinforce this or that attitude of the group, some may not. As we shall have occasion to discuss the problem of authority in the arts later in this essay, no more will be said at this juncture save to indicate that "good" art is precisely the sort of art which lends itself most readily to aesthetic perception and the aesthetic emotions. We have developed a critical tradition that provides us with viable criteria for determining what art of the past can be called "good." In other words, aesthetic education does not reject the desirability of "enjoyment" in aesthetic experience; nor does it deny that works of art should arouse emotion. The enjoyment and the emotion, however, are not identical with what the use of these terms in ordinary discourse and everyday experience denotes, although they could not exist or develop without roots in that experience.

The key to both aesthetic pleasure and aesthetic emotion, it seems to me, is the dramatic structure of the aesthetic object. Drama arouses emotion and gives us pleasure in contemplating the emotion so aroused. But, one may ask, whence comes this fascination with dramatic structure? Why does it command our attention even in such abstract forms as the tensions, conflicts, and resolutions in a musical composition or an abstract painting? Because, as has been pointed out, life itself is dynamic and be-

---

[11] As in so many other notions, Plato has proved to be most challenging and educative when he confronts us with a principle that we feel to be wrong. We resist, for example, the idea of censoring art, but has anyone found a way of teaching values without discriminating among them? And has anyone found a way of teaching the young without imposing some things on them without their rational assent?

cause imagination can convert the dynamism of nature into a drama. It is by means of imagination that we are put in suspense as to the outcome of a process. In nature there are no surprises; only when imagination raises the possibility of things being otherwise do we slip to the edge of the chair awaiting the outcome — which according to the laws of nature couldn't be otherwise.

I am quite sure that this attempt at describing aesthetic enjoyment is far from successful, but it had to be undertaken because unless the peculiar essence of aesthetic enjoyment is noted — even if not articulated verbally or conceptually — aesthetic education may go wrong in several ways. One way lies in using aesthetic materials not for their intrinsic value but solely as instrumental to other extra-aesthetic ones. Art may become an instrument of propaganda in behalf of this or that ideology. This is an especially insidious kind of social conditioning because it works through perception and is consequently hard to resist. Wary as one may be of the influence of images, it is still difficult for most people to *see* long-haired young men in tattered jeans as decent citizens. They don't look citizenlike, and they must prove that they are.

A similar misuse of aesthetic education is to employ it solely as a means of enriching other subjects of instruction. In some schools painting, poetry, and architecture are used to liven up the social studies. Properly used, aesthetic materials could afford the pupil a rare perception of historical periods and styles of culture. Thus the *Iliad* enables us to see the world as the poets of that time perceived it. This sort of perception is quite different from the understanding of a culture through verbal descriptions of its institutions, wars, politics, or daily life. The misuse I have in mind, on the contrary, uses works of art to illustrate the verbal materials, i.e., as visual aids.

Another kind of going wrong in aesthetic education divorces the aesthetic experience from all other value experience and exempts it from all standards. In school this can take the form of just "doing things" with paint, clay, or dance as the mood of the pupil dictates. Art becomes a totally subjective phenomenon, a doing of one's thing — any thing — so long as it is one's own. Art is always the result of someone doing "his thing," but art is always an objectification of feeling, and once objectified, it enters into the public domain and cannot avoid the judgment of those who view it. Art would be useless if it had no effects on extra-aesthetic values, but it would be otiose if it did not have a peculiarly individual quality that was not duplicated in any other mode of experience.

There is no reason to be overly rigid in these matters, but we should respect the peculiar sort of enjoyment and satisfaction that can properly be expected from the aesthetic object and from no other. Art cannot do for us what science or technology or religion or friendship can do, but none of these can do what art can do. If it seems to the layman on the school board that so delicate and transient a satisfaction as comes from contemplation of the aesthetic image is not sufficiently important to warrant a place in the curriculum or the budget, then it must be made as clear as possible that most if not all of our value judgments are powerfully influenced by aesthetic judgments. The appearances of things do make a difference in our choices, perhaps a more powerful difference than information and reasoning.

In closing this section of the essay, one must reiterate that although aesthetic education will have indirect effects on all other realms of value, there is no guarantee that it will bolster the kind of value commitments that would make most parents comfortable. We do not guarantee the social effects of teaching "good" science; rather, we are satisfied when the pupil develops his powers of thinking as good scientists do. The situation is no different with aesthetic education. The goal is the development of ways of perceiving aesthetic images as do those who by experience and reflection have become connoisseurs. That this development will lead to enlightened cherishing requires the same sort of faith in the value of cultivation as does all schooling.

III

Education for Enlightened Cherishing

W HAT sort of schooling is needed for enlightened cherishing?
Knowledge contributes to enlightenment, but the knowledge that
enlightens cherishing includes both scientific knowledge and value
knowledge. Without adequate scientific knowledge men choose
ineptly, not only the means to ends but often the ends themselves. Even when our knowledge of means and consequences is
quite adequate, lives still go awry, presumably because we cherish
the wrong things or misconstrue their importance relative to ourselves or to each other. Knowledge for enlightened cherishing is
sometimes called wisdom, which combines knowledge of human
nature with clear-headedness about what can and cannot be ac-
complished.

The humanities traditionally have been regarded as the source
of wisdom, especially of insight into human nature and the styles
of life that facilitate or inhibit happiness. The renewed interest
in the humanities is, I believe, the result of bewilderment about
what *humanitas,* or the essence of humanity, is. We no longer
know how to define it, and some doubt that it can be defined.
Erwin Panofsky notes that in classical times *humanitas* had to do
with man's difference from and presumable superiority to the
animals and barbarians, who behaved like animals (*barbaritas*).
In the Middle Ages *humanitas* was defined in terms of man's

inferiority to God, and in the Renaissance *humanitas* dealt with both superiority and inferiority more or less simultaneously.[1]

What, then, is the proper meaning of *humanitas* in our time? Shall it celebrate our superiority to the animals? But in our time there is despair about our ability to transform the crudity of animal impulse. There is even greater despair about undoing the perversions of human achievements by the misuse of intelligence and imagination that have perpetrated unspeakable cruelties. How can we define the "human" essence by its superiority to the animals when blatant pornography, sadism, and surrender to the immediate push us closer not merely to the animal but to the depraved animal? Are we to define humanity as being lower than the animal? And if we try to define man as inferior to God and angels, we are told that the new freedom in religion questions not only the dogmas and the practices of the church but the very existence of God. If we cannot distinguish ourselves from animals or God, then the Renaissance stance toward humanity is no longer available to us.

In the minds of the school-board member, the parent, the newspaper editor, and the legislator the role of the humanities is to teach values. But what values, whose values, and by what right? These are no longer academic questions. For example, consider the school's predicament with respect to the redemption of the disadvantaged. The schools are to redeem the victims of racism and poverty but not, we are told, by imposing middle-class values upon them. However, if one asks in what way the disadvantaged are disadvantaged, we are told that they lack the means to achieve what seem suspiciously like middle-class values. Do the humanities transcend class-bound values? Granted the desire of the public for the school to have another go at value edu-

[1] Erwin Panofsky, *Meaning in the Visual Arts* (New York: Doubleday, 1955); from the chapter "The History of Art as a Humanistic Discipline," reprinted in Ralph A. Smith, ed., *Aesthetics and Criticism in Art Education* (Chicago: Rand McNally, 1966), pp. 215-216.

cation, why pick on the humanities? Why not the social studies, civics, the problems of democracy, interdisciplinary studies, working among the poor?

Perhaps the answer lies in a comment that Werner Jaeger, the author of *Paideia,* once made: when in deep trouble, western man seems to turn to the ideal of humanity that had its birth in classical times. The ideal was reinvoked in the Middle Ages and again in the Renaissance. This may be a historical accident or an example of racial memory, but it may be that the belief of the classical humanist that the essence of humanity does not change is hard to destroy. There is a sense in which the generic virtues that define that essence do not change, because they are the very criteria, linguistically and conceptually, by which we classify entities as human, nonhuman, and inhuman. There can be, and indeed there must be, new behavioral forms with which to act out the virtues in every epoch, but once the virtues themselves are challenged, we have the kind of anxiety that has bemused us since the end of World War I.

The ideal of the humanities quite naturally suggests the humanistic studies, the studies which deal with virtue and wisdom. There is a long string of testimonials from Erasmus to Matthew Arnold that the study of letters, especially *belles lettres,* humanizes man as no other studies can. Moreover, despite serious setbacks, the humanities still command academic respect and harmonize with the hymn of excellence that resounded in so many educational conferences during the last decade. For these reasons, among others, the humanities have been urged as a means of restoring respect for the human essence and value education.

The life outcome anticipated from the humanities course is some sort of value commitment, the introjection of some set of norms that will guide the person forever after in his choices. The school outcomes — those which might be discernible at the end of the course — are distinctive habits of perceiving, imagining, and thinking, forms of feeling and willing that have been disciplined by the study of the humanities. The humanities course, therefore, should not aim at adding to the pupil's empirical knowledge about the cosmos, man, and his culture. The sciences are the proper repositories of such knowledge, and the humanities are not good substitutes for the sciences.

Yet many of the courses in the high-school curriculum are humanistic only in the sense that they give the student *knowledge* about cherishing: many appreciation courses, survey courses in the history of civilizations, most history courses, and not a few literature courses are in this category. If this charge is well founded, then something other than this mode of instruction is justified, either by new courses or by reorganization of old ones that will stress the shaping of taste rather than the imparting of knowledge. If enlightened cherishing is the distinctive contribution of the humanities course to the outcomes of schooling, it should guide the choice of materials and approach so as not to lose this distinctiveness.

It seems to me that a simple revival of the classical literary curriculum is out of the question. For one thing it would entail a revival of the study of the classical languages, an extremely unlikely development. For another, the notion that a few Latin and Greek authors have crystallized all worthwhile knowledge makes sense only on a very narrow notion of "worthwhile." The reinstatement of the humanities as a study of *belles lettres* would involve the course in jurisdictional disputes with literature courses of various kinds that are now in the curriculum. Historical and philosophical materials that would qualify for the humanities are already in the anthologies for literature courses or courses in the history of ideas or cultural history. As for the humanities becoming a kind of allied arts course, this, too, encounters the fact that music and visual art are already represented in the curriculum. These considerations seem to suggest that the most promising direction for the humanities course is to approach value education through aesthetic education.[2]

How does aesthetic education contribute to enlightened cherishing? That depends, of course, on how one conceives of aesthetic education. The view advocated in this essay is that aesthetic education is first of all the training of imaginative perception to enable the pupil to apprehend sensory content, formed into an image that expresses some feeling quality. So stated, aesthetic education does not concern itself with propagandizing for any specific ideology or way of life. On the contrary, its first concern is that the pupil become adept in contemplating images of feeling which works of art present to us.

The effect of such education on cherishing is therefore indirect, largely by broadening and differentiating the repertoire of feeling. This is important because most human troubles are caused by oversimplified emotional responses. Consider, for example, the miseries inflicted on mankind by the oversimplification of love. Love is not a single emotion but, rather, a complex sentiment in which jealousy, fear, anger, joy, and elation are so intertwined that poets and dramatists have never given up the task of unraveling it. Nevertheless, most marriages, in our country at any rate, are stumbled into by young people to whom love is a many-splendored thing, the most splendored of which is a strong feeling of mutual attraction. The disastrous consequences of this oversimplification are notorious.

Another instance of the destructiveness of raw emotion is anger, with its biological complement of aggression. Our primitive emotions, mediated by the autonomic nervous system, are

[2] For further discussion of this thesis, see Harry S. Broudy, *Building a Philosophy of Education* (Englewood Cliffs, N.J.: Prentice-Hall, 1961), Chapter 13, and Broudy, B. O. Smith, and J. R. Burnett, *Democracy and Excellence in American Secondary Education* (Chicago: Rand McNally, 1964), Chapter 13. Also see Broudy, "The Role of the Humanities in the Curriculum," *Journal of Aesthetic Education* 1, no. 2 (1966): 17-29.

admirably suited to survival in the jungle. Since few of us now live in jungles, the autonomic nervous system that triggers violent lust, fear, and rage is something we could well do without. Stuck with this emotional apparatus but unable to act out his emotions by attacking the enemy or fleeing, man used imagination to devise symbolic outlets for his drives. Insult, satire, the snide remark, facial and bodily gestures can all be used to express anger indirectly. However, in modifying the response, the emotion itself is changed: the snide remark mirrors not violent rage but another and more elusive form of anger. A vast portion of poetry, drama, fiction, and indeed of all the arts is devoted to inventing or portraying an almost infinite assortment of feelings that have spun off from the basic raw emotions as imagination was brought to bear on them.

The quality of life is measured by the repertory of feeling which pervades it. Life is rich if the repertory of feelings is large and the discrimination among them fine. Life is coarse, brutish, and violent when the repertory is meager and undifferentiated. Aesthetic education's role in enlightened cherishing is to enlarge and refine the repertory of feeling. Moral reflection, critical thinking, and knowledge about the world also contribute to the enlightenment of cherishing, but aesthetic experience does its work in the domain of feeling, to enlighten us about the nature of feeling.

Plato in the *Republic* makes much of the need to *learn* to love and hate wisely, and he notes that dogs are wise in that they distinguish between friends and strangers. Unenlightened cherishing shows up in the inappropriate emotional response. Courage, for example, as the name of a general attitude, means standing up to danger, but we would want to distinguish courage from rashness and brashness, and the differences lie in understanding the nature of the danger and one's resources for dealing with it. Where do we get our cues as to what is the appropriate emotional response?

The most frequent source of models for our emotional response is the group stereotype. The group makes pretty clear what is expected in the standard situations, and all the social institutions, including the popular arts, line up to reinforce these expectations. And so the little boy fights the bully twice his size regardless of consequences, and the mobster maintains his silence despite all evidence that he has been betrayed. We may judge these responses as unintelligent, but we respect these simple reactions because they signify a kind of emotional honesty, whereas too finely cultivated distinctions may result in hypocrisy and self-serving rationalizations.

Is conforming to group expectations the path to enlightened cherishing? In a minimal sense it is, for presumably the group has survived by means of these responses. Furthermore, no group of any size can function very long unless it does develop stereotypes for standard situations. Conventional feelings and moral judgments are the flywheels of society; they sustain its momentum amid local and momentary fluctuations. As to the individual deviations, some are so nonadaptive that they are eliminated, but some raise questions about the stereotypes themselves, and still others furnish possible alternatives to the stereotypes. The laws, statutory and biological, take care of the first kind; philosophy is concerned with the second; and the creative artist on occasion helps us with the third.

The resources for making cherishing more enlightened, broadly speaking, are found in the total cultural heritage. Everything in that heritage — science, religion, technology, art, philosophy — is, in one sense or another, relevant to wisdom. Nevertheless, such a poem as that of Yeats on old age or such a painting as Grant Wood's *American Gothic* is much closer to the cherishing aspect of life than is a treatise on high-energy physics. The scientific culture, to choose one of C. P. Snow's pair of cultures, is one of the great shapers of value possibility, of what values men can actualize as well as the means of their actualization. Yet in the last reckoning the pattern of our choosing is not a scientific matter nor one that we would leave to a computer calculating odds on alternative possibilities. The pattern of our choosing *is our Self,* so that the knowledge most relevant to cherishing is that part of the cultural heritage that is primarily concerned with Selves, those elusive entities which men endlessly lose and search for. The humanities, or Snow's literary culture, are our prime source for the record of man's experiments with cherishing — wisely and otherwise.

Over long stretches of time men of cultivation have achieved substantial consensus on conduct that makes life good and happy, and there is a sense in which this consensus has a presumptive validity for the *educated* man. Many who counsel a return to the humanities accept the Hellenistic-Judeo-Christian image of conduct as a positive guide for the rearing of the young and for the conduct of society as a whole. They would inculcate it without skepticism about its relevance for our times. This is a brave but impossible ploy. I would suggest that there is a criterion of value which is both more modest and more fundamental than Aristotle's magnanimous man, or the Christian gentleman of the Renaissance, or the cultured humanist of the Victorian era. This criterion is the process of cultivation itself.

APPROACHES TO AESTHETIC EDUCATION

I shall argue that as a matter of policy, strategy, and tactics, aesthetic education ought to concentrate on helping the pupil to perceive works of art, the environment, nature, clothing, etc. in the way that artists in the respective media tend to perceive them. This is not to say that aesthetic perception is the only proper form of perception or that education is to concern itself only with aesthetic perception. In opting for perception as the proper focus for aesthetic education, I am rejecting — with certain qualification — two others: one is the performance approach and the other is the traditional course in appreciation of music, art, literature, etc.

The Performance Approach

For the most part aesthetic education in the public schools has consisted of instruction in music and art or, as it used to be called, drawing. I shall not go into the history of these developments or the rationale offered for them.[3] The performance approach initiates the pupil into skills of a particular art. The skill is formed by practice under guidance, and typically in music and art the guidance is furnished by a supervisor and to some extent in the elementary school by the classroom teacher. In the secondary school the arts are taught by specialists. Although literature is the one art required of all pupils throughout the twelve years of schooling, it is not ordinarily included under aesthetic education, perhaps because it is not often taught as an art form.

The justification for the performance approach is twofold. First, acquiring the skill in school may induce the pupil to exercise it in later years, perhaps as a talented amateur; in any event it augments a person's accomplishments. The second justification is that art and music classes in school spot youngsters with talent who might go on to become professional performers.

Both goals and justifications are defensible. Were it not for this form of aesthetic education, far fewer of our citizens could read musical notation or play some musical instrument. And while analogous skills in the visual arts are harder to identify, it is fair to say that the fear of trying one's hand at painting and sculpture, as amateur pursuits, has been greatly mitigated by the freer methods of teaching art. These approaches stress the importance

[3] For a general view of the development of art education in American schools, the reader is referred to Fred Logan's *The Growth of Art in American Schools* (New York: Harper and Brothers, 1955) and Eliot Eisner's chapter "American Education and the Future of Art Education" in *Art Education,* Sixty-fourth Yearbook of the National Society for the Study of Education, Part II (1965).

of expressing oneself in paint, clay, etc. without regard to rules or criteria of quality. In abandoning the rules, however, the school is doing only what avant-garde artists in general have been urging all along. It would be ridiculous to enforce standards in the school that articulate artists scorn.

The inadequacies of the performance approach outweigh, I am afraid, its very solid benefits. For one thing, most pupils do not elect to continue their art studies in high school, so that at the very time when adolescents are caught up in maelstroms of feeling, whatever aid the arts could give them is no longer available, at least not in formal schoolwork. In the second place, creative writing, drama, dance, and films are not generally available either in the elementary or secondary grades, and yet these media are rich sources of aesthetic experience. Finally, as regards the talented youngster, the earlier he can get started in professional studio training the better. For example, ballet as a career has to be started at quite an early age. The public school should not be expected to furnish such highly specialized professional training as part of the required program in general education.

For these reasons, one might argue that the performance approach in all the standard media should be used only during the elementary years, grades K-6. If we are careful in our use of the word "language," we can say that just as the child becomes literate in ordinary language during these years, so should he also become literate in the "languages" of the various art media. And one should urge that these skills be given the same attention as other tool subjects of the curriculum, not used to fill in the dead spots before recess or the dismissal bell.

A major reason for insisting on performance training in the various arts is that without some experience in the medium it is difficult, albeit not impossible, to learn to perceive properly in that medium. As Bernard Bosanquet has insisted[4] and every

[4] *Three Lectures on the Aesthetic* (London: Macmillan, 1915), Chapter II.

artist will attest, each medium has its own resources of expression. We cannot express in marble what we can express with paint or through musical tones. One does not have to become a proficient painter to appreciate the opportunities and limitations of oils, water colors, and collages, but unless one has tried to paint, he will find incomprehensible why some paintings, e.g., frescoes, have the effects they do have. And the same is true in all of the other media.

However, it is one thing to have children work in a medium to acquire real proficiency in it — even on a decent amateur level — and it is another to work under guidance in various media to get the feel of their expressive powers, their sensory potentialities, and their formal properties. The first six years of schooling (or seven, including a year of kindergarten), with at least a period every day for such work, might have a fair chance of teaching the rudiments of aesthetic "literacy." One may assume that during these years there will be no dearth of opportunity to perceive aesthetic objects, but one might defend primary emphasis on performance skills during this period.

In this connection one wonders why the self-contained classroom, if it is to continue as the paradigm for elementary education, cannot be taught by teachers who are themselves (as generally educated persons as well as by virtue of their teacher training) able to give the performance instruction, remembering, of course, that it is performance not for the sake of performance but, rather, for the sake of proper perception. What sort of teacher training it would take to bring the elementary classroom teacher up to this level of competence is subject for another inquiry. As things stand, however, the more or less standard brand of elementary teacher, by virtue of neither general education nor teacher training, is either competent enough or confident enough to undertake performance training, and certainly not in more than one medium. Some sort of team teaching is the most likely answer for at least another generation.

At the secondary level performance courses in the diverse arts still have a place — about the same as they now occupy, viz., as electives — but for reasons already adduced, it is difficult to defend them as *required* components of general education.

Aesthetic Education as Appreciation

The customary alternative to the conventional skill training is the typical course in appreciation of music, painting, or literature. The one in music, for example, analyzes various styles of composition in selected periods of musical history, e.g., the concerto form, rondo, march, and chorale. A typical instance of each style or composer is played as an illustration of the analysis. Something is said about the life of the composer and what the critics think of him. To test his learning in the course, the student is asked to recall certain items of knowledge about the music and possibly to identify a composition from a sample or to comment on its stylistic characteristics. Because of time limitations, the number of compositions dealt with in the course is necessarily limited, and since the course is usually elective, it is a matter of chance whether the student takes more than one such appreciation course in music or in arts other than music.

Such courses, well taught, have much to commend them. *Knowing about* the masterpieces of music or painting, being able to recognize their stylistic characteristics, knowing something about the artists and the great developments in art history — these are valuable additions to one's education. Yet it is doubtful that such appreciation courses affect in a fundamental way the aesthetic life of the student. *Knowing about* art, unless accompanied by a very rich and copious amount of aesthetic perception, may not change the fabric of our life any more than reading about the life of St. Francis of Assisi automatically makes us saintly or reading about the works of Isaac Newton and Albert Einstein makes our thinking more scientific.

I am far from wanting to denigrate knowledge about the arts or about anything else, for that matter. On the contrary, given the ability to perceive the aesthetic image, knowledge deepens and broadens the satisfaction that accrues from such perception. A connoisseur (buff) of anything not only wants to engage in the activity but is incurably eager to know all there is to know about it. So let us refrain from sneering at knowledge about this or that, as the more feverish advocates of direct experience in education are wont to do. Nonetheless, *knowledge about* is no substitute for the *perception of,* as the standard appreciation courses so often are taken to be.

The most serious consequence of substituting *knowledge about* for *experience of* art is that one's standards tend to become conventional. One feels obliged to say that Beethoven is great because authorities cited in the course said so. The Fifth Symphony is a masterpiece because Beethoven wrote it, and Beethoven was a great composer because he wrote the Fifth Symphony. This is the sort of question-begging pronouncement that appreciation courses are likely to beget in the student whose own experience has been too meager or too unreflective to develop tastes and standards of his own. Enlightened cherishing means not only liking X or Y or Z but also being able to point to those features of X, Y, and Z by virtue of which one can defend the judgment that X, Y, and Z deserve to be liked.

But clearly if one has had no or very scant experience with X, Y, and Z, one is hardly able to form an authentic judgment about them. It is only when he has experienced X, Y, and Z and many other items of the same sort, only when he has studied what critics have said in terms of his own experience, that he can judge for himself whether X, Y, and Z have the features that constitute goodness in art. The right to make such judgments presupposes the ability to defend them by virtue of the experience and of serious reflection upon that experience. We can like what we like; there is no disputing about that. But about the right to make judgments one can indeed dispute; one must have the appropriate credentials.

I have tried in this section to elucidate the meaning of enlightened cherishing and to suggest the sort of schooling that would promote it. The humanities are the disciplines most closely related to value formation and commitment, but although the fine arts are included in the humanities, their role in value education has been neither adequately examined nor exploited. The arts represent the aesthetic component of the humanities, and there is no reason why the humanities must be confined to the works of the remote past. The effect of the arts on enlightened cherishing is indirect so far as specific values are concerned, but it is very direct in that it has an immediate impact on the feeling repertoire of the person. The perceptual approach to aesthetic education is a viable alternative to both the performance and the appreciation approaches, and it promises a way of evading, as much as one can, the dilemma of abandoning standards altogether or imposing them on the young arbitrarily.

IV

Aesthetic Education as Perception

Oᴺᴇ of the major obstacles to aesthetic education that purports to go beyond proficiency in some art medium is a suspicion that it would result in an amorphous mixture of vague ingredients. On first encountering the notion, teachers ask, "What is it about?," "How do you go about it?," "How can you test the results of the instruction?" To offer some assurance that aesthetic education can be reasonably systematic and definite and the results, to a large extent, testable, it will be necessary to translate the dimensions of the aesthetic image discussed in Section II into educational terms.

PERCEPTION OF SENSORY QUALITIES

Each medium in which works of art are produced has its own complement of sensory qualities: sounds, colors, shapes, words, gestures. Each modality (type of sensory quality) has variations. Sounds differ in pitch, volume, timbre; colors vary in hue, saturation, and brightness. The first requisite for good aesthetic perception is sensitivity to a wide range of sensory qualities and their variations. For example, it is a familiar psychological fact that we tend to perceive a familiar object such as a table top or a window shade as uniform in color. Thus we speak of the sheet of paper on the desk in front of us as white, even though the variations of light make it unlikely that it will be of a uniform color as far as the image on the retina is concerned. However, if our attention is called to the variations — as paintings often do — we note them. Under special circumstances we can discern differences that under standard conditions we simply ignore. In aesthetic education we have to adopt the attitude that perceiving the variations in sensory quality of the object is important. This comes out when we try to copy a painting or play a musical composition. We are forced to notice everything in the model in the greatest detail, and although faithful copying is not held in high artistic repute, pedagogically it is an effective way of fixing the roving eye on what is there to be sensed.

Part of the difference between a cultivated taste and an uncultivated one is simply the number and fineness of sensory discriminations that are made in the aesthetic image. The novice sees very little of what is there — he tends to see the sheet of paper as white, the blanket of snow as white, the wash on the line as white. He hears the main melody of a piece and responds to the main rhythm. Small variations of tone and rhythm, of hue and brightness, he ignores. The cultivated observer can spend an hour on a segment of a work of art that commands no more than a flick of the eye or prick of the ear from the novice.

Of course we do not perceive patches of red or green or single tones as such. They come to us already patterned, and when we try to improve our sensory discrimination, it is the variations in the patterns of sounds and colors to which we attend. With practice we detect a greater number of patterns, and the number of them to which we can attend simultaneously increases also. At the beginning, for example, it takes our full attention to follow the melodic line from one set of instruments to another while listening to the orchestra, but in time we can hear the melodic lines and accompaniments simultaneously in a number of instruments. Our perception span expands to apprehend larger and larger clusters of sensory stimuli.

This is no more than to say that in aesthetic perception, as in any other kind, the pattern is the unit and not an isolated sensation of color or sound. Pattern, however, is part of what we mean by form; hence we perceive both the sensory and formal properties — and the expressive as well — in a unitary perception. Why, then, speak of training in the sensory dimension as if the sensory components could or should be perceived without the others?

We do so because in order to improve any performance, we diagnose the blocks to progress. Although the bodily organism works as a whole, when it gets out of kilter, we seek a particular organ that is dysfunctioning and try to fix that. For example, the cause of a pupil's indifferent progress may lie in the inability or disinclination of the pupil to keep his attention on the object. At such a juncture we may very well draw his attention to variations in color and sound patterns because if he does attend, it may facilitate the perception of the formal and expressive properties of the object. I realize that some educational theorists abhor analysis as destructive of wholeness. Holism is fine when the organism is functioning well; when it is not, taking the process apart and treating the parts separately is often the only recourse. Not to do so would be like forbidding the surgeon to remove a diseased appendix on the ground that it would do violence to the wholeness of the body function, that somehow it is unnatural to put asunder what nature hath joined together. Although the aesthetic experience is a unity of sensory content, form, and expressiveness, we can abstract each one of them for our special attention when we need to do so to carry on aesthetic education.

PERCEPTION OF FORMAL PROPERTIES

As has already been indicated, the formal properties of the aesthetic image can refer to the tiniest of patterns, e.g., three notes, a triangle, the curve of a dancer's arms, or they can refer to the story line of a play or to the development of a character, a symphony, or even a series of compositions such as the operas comprising Wagner's *Ring*. DeWitt H. Parker reduces the characteristics of aesthetic form to the principle of organic unity, or unity in variety; the principle of the theme; the principle of thematic variations; balance; the principle of hierarchy, and evolution, although he does not include hierarchy as one of the irreducible types of aesthetic unity.[1]

We have already mentioned the first principle, that of unity in variety. Roughly it means that the distinguishable units or elements seem to belong to each other. The most obvious way of belonging is that each contributes something to the functioning of the whole, e.g., as the heart, liver, and brain all contribute something essential but different to the life of the body. When elements are so related, each part needs the whole to give it meaning and vice versa; it is an organic relation. The heart is not a heart until its contribution to the body is understood.

What is the criterion for successful unification in a work of art? In a machine we make the test by removing a part at a time to see what happens or fails to happen. It is the same in the human body; we try to trace malfunction to a specific part of the body. But it is not easy to say just what difference removing five bars of music from a musical composition makes or trimming several inches from a painting. In recent years some artists have sliced up their canvases without disturbing their "unity." To be sure, after the artist has completed the work and it has been around for a considerable length of time, removing an element or displacing it will strike us as destroying its unity, but it is to be doubted that we would feel the discordance had we been shown the work with the part missing in the first place.

Given all the sketches that an artist had made for a given painting or a composer for a certain score, how many of even the enlightened critics would have chosen the same final version

[1] DeWitt H. Parker, *The Analysis of Art* (New Haven, Conn.: Yale University Press, 1926).

as did the artist? Since the function of the work of art is itself not something which is unambiguous, it is a dubious business to try to guess what this patch of color or that shape contributed to that function. Nevertheless, harmony and lack of it are perceived and cannot be dismissed simply because observers do not always agree on what constitutes it.

Unity in works of art is more likely to be tested by finding common elements in the various parts. When a melody is repeated, it binds the flow of the music together. When rhythms have partial similarity, when a color is distributed throughout a picture, they contribute to unity. As Parker points out, the five principles he cited are means to organic unity, and they are based on the repetition of some common element in one fashion or another; even contrast depends on some similarity. Thus the principle of the theme and the principle of variations on the theme use partial repetition: recurrence, transposition of the theme, variation of the theme in size or duration, alternation of two themes, and the inversion of themes.

Balance is another of Parker's principles that contributes to unity. He defines it as the "equality of opposing or contrasting elements," but the opposing elements need each other and together create a unity. Even in symmetrical balance, Parker notes, there is opposition, because the elements are in opposite direction, right or left, up or down. But it is important to stress that balance can be of almost any elements: shapes may balance each other, but so can colors and degrees of importance. It takes a number of ordinary figures to balance the interest which the king in a picture commands. We need not recount the variations in balance that artists have used and will create. In aesthetic education the point is not to catalogue types of balance or to memorize them but, rather, to form the habit of becoming sensitive to them in a wide variety of media.

Rhythm, according to Parker, is based on thematic variation and balance, for rhythm is a repetition of stresses, but the stresses or accents balance each other. There has to be a balance between the beat on the drum and the interval of silence that makes the beat effective.

By evolution as a principle of aesthetic unity Parker means the process of earlier phases determining later ones. He distinguishes the dramatic type of evolution from the nondramatic one. I have already stressed the former, and I have indicated my opinion that this is the most expressive form of aesthetic organization. The cumulative climactic nature of dramatic evolution generates suspense, concentrates meaning, and holds interest as nothing else does. One might say that all the other principles of unity listed by Parker, e.g., thematic variation or balance, can themselves be dramatic or nondramatic. The nondramatic type of evolution has no special climax, no special event that unifies the antecedents and the consequences. There is an unfolding but with "no obvious high points."

The Parker classification of formal principles makes it possible to carry on formal analysis of aesthetic objects more or less systematically. Themes and variations, balances of various types, rhythmic patterns, and the like can be identified, pointed out, and talked about, and that is of the first importance for instruction and testing the results of instruction.

One cannot repeat too often that in the perceptual approach to aesthetic education verbal descriptions and categories are used as guides to perceiving the object. It is not sufficient to tell the class that this picture or that musical composition has balance or evolution; the pupil has to see the balance and hear the evolution in definite works of art. Furthermore, aesthetic analysis is not undertaken for the sake of analysis or for the purpose of giving students a chance to air their knowledge about works of art. Analysis is done for the sake of better perception. Occasionally an aesthetic image makes its impact on us at once as a whole. A brilliant sunset, a quiet brook, a musical phrase, a beautiful face — each is perceived as such, and that's the end of it; no breaking up of the image, no analysis, is needed.

Unfortunately, complex works of art and even our natural environment do not impinge upon us so simply and directly. Their impact on us is more like hearing a foreign tongue for the first time: everything seems to have been run together, we cannot detect any pattern or phrasing, and so it makes no sense, even if we have some familiarity with the written language. But we know that the speaker does make sense to his compatriots, and we know that these compatriots do not translate word for word but, rather, apprehend patterns of meaning in the flow of discourse. Similarly, aesthetic experience can be confusing until we catch on to its "phrasing," so to speak. The principles of formal organization describe some of the ways in which the aesthetic image is phrased or patterned; analysis merely helps us to discern the patterns more readily.

It is not even of prime importance that everyone in the class agree as to just what formal properties are being perceived or which were intended by the artist. But unless the pupils get the swing of the rhythm, recognize the plot of the play, sense the thematic variations in music or a story, they are not having *an* experience, certainly not an aesthetic one. Questioning artists, one learns that it is the formal properties of art that interest them most often. Painters tend to see objects as potential compositions for a picture, writers perceive persons and events in their potential for a story. A painter passing a group of children at play in the ghetto and a sociologist and a social worker passing the same group at the same time will perceive it differently. The sociologist sees the children as examples of the social structure of the ghetto; the social worker sees them as children to be "helped"; and the painter, as a painter, may see them as elements in a composition of color and shapes which may capture the special spirit of children at play. In aesthetic education one tries to have the pupil perceive (at least some of the time) the world as artists in the various media do.

PERCEPTION OF EXPRESSIVENESS

I think it takes no great effort to convince anyone that training to perceive the sensory and formal properties of aesthetic experience is possible. Nor is there any insuperable difficulty in devising tests for progress in developing sensitivity in these dimensions. Even those educators who grimly determine to package experience into bundles of behavioral objectives can be satisfied, for discrimination of sensory materials and various types of formal order can be defined behaviorally.

As for the training itself, it requires no more than examining aesthetic objects under guidance and encouraging the pupil to make the required discriminations either alone or with others. The basic ground rule for these exercises is that all who participate in them be ready to point to something in the object by virtue of which they are willing to assert that it has this or that property or characteristic. What could be more behavioral? There is also nothing to prevent the teacher from having the pupil make his own aesthetic objects to serve as targets for perception. In this way performance training and perception training coalesce. The performer and the maker use perception from moment to moment to test whether the effects they desire are being achieved. Indeed, John Dewey and some of his latter-day disciples insist that artistic creation is a kind of problem-solving in which aesthetic "qualities" rather than concepts are the counters. I confess to considerable skepticism about the validity of this aesthetic analogue to cognitive problem-solving, but it can be used profitably at some stages of aesthetic analysis.

For example, the distinction between the sensory and formal properties of the aesthetic image can be brought out more clearly if we vary one dimension at a time. We can arrange ten spots of orange color in a number of ways, or we can take any one of the patterns and give it a variety of colors or color combinations. Melodies can be held constant while rhythms are changed; rhythms can be held constant while the orchestration is varied. Sometimes works of art can be selected to bring out these distinctions, but this entails fairly laborious research; it is easier to contrive materials which are sure to do so. However, the plethora of collections of art reproductions now available in the various media makes the task of selecting materials for the study of the various dimensions of the aesthetic experience far easier than it used to be.

Once the principle of the perceptual approach is understood, the devices for exploiting it can be left to the teacher, for if anything should be left to her discretion, this is it. There are so many possibilities for choice in the materials to be used that a fair test of whether the whole approach has been understood is the flexibility of the teacher in applying it.

However, the teaching situation is radically changed when we come to the expressive dimension of aesthetic experience. We can still use the perceptual approach, but we can no longer say with confidence just what it is that is to be perceived or how we train pupils to perceive it. Colors and shapes are fairly public objects, and given normal sense organs, there is little difficulty in getting agreement on whether a given area of color is red, green, or violet. The same, of course, is true in the fields of sounds and gestures. But suppose that a seascape is said to depict an angry sea or a melody is said to be cheerful and spritely or a poem melancholy. To what in the aesthetic object do we direct the attention of the observers as evidence for our characterization? And if, as has been stressed, aesthetic images express not merely the gross emotions but also an indefinite range of feeling, then instructing others in the expressive dimension becomes problematic indeed.

And yet, if we are true to the principle of phenomenological objectivity, the expressiveness of the image must be perceived as being *in* the image, not as something the image causes us to recollect which we then add to it. The principle of phenomenological objectivity does not require us to prove that the quality of feeling being expressed must have originated in the object or that it is physically part of the object. The principle requires only that the quality expressed must be *perceived as being in the object*. So any education with regard to expressiveness must also begin with perception.

I would suggest that for aesthetic education, at least in the form to which most public-school pupils might be exposed to it, we do not make the expressive dimension a direct object of instruction. This may sound strange in view of the generally accepted idea that the expressive dimension is the most important of all — that for the sake of which artists labor to give formal order to the sensory contents. Yet this result is not so paradoxical as it may first appear.

In the first place, if the artist has been successful, and if the pupil has perceived the sensory and formal components fully, i.e., as carefully and completely as at that stage of development he has been able to do, then the expressive qualities will have been perceived also. This, I take it, is what we mean by a successful aesthetic image. If the meaning has not come through, then we must charge it to lack of experience on the part of the student or to failure of the artist, and neither of these, at any given moment, can be corrected by instruction. It is quite reasonable to direct the pupil's attention to the sensory properties in a work of art and to have him say, "Oh, yes, I see that the snow is violet, not white." But would we want him to say, "I didn't perceive the cheerfulness of this painting, but now that you mention it, I do perceive it"? Perhaps, but only if he really does perceive it.

There is no expressiveness without sensory materials formally arranged, but there can be sensory content formally organized which is not expressive — as a metaphor. Books arranged in alphabetical order or by size might be an example. We speak of works done by artists that do not seem to have any life, although technically they are competent enough. In music the technically competent performer who lacks expressiveness is, unfortunately, not an uncommon phenomenon. We cannot abstract the expressive dimension as we can the sensory and the formal ones, and because we cannot do so, there is no handle by which we can grasp either the artist's or the pupil's difficulty with expressiveness.

In the second place, the difficulty has less to do with whether the pupil perceives any message or meaning or expressiveness but with whether there is *one* message that all must perceive. It is this latter requirement that we cannot hope to fill in aesthetic education. With regard to this point, two remarks are in order. One is that agreement on the meaning of any given aesthetic image is not especially crucial to the goals of aesthetic education as we have described and discussed them. If the development of value potentials through contemplation of feeling is the goal, then whether or not one perceives some expressiveness in the image is more important than that all observers agree on what the meaning is. When dealing with works of art that have survived a long critical tradition and have been interpreted by experts over long periods of time, there is some sense in comparing what we take to be the meaning expressed with those of the tradition. Those who proceed in aesthetic education beyond the basic rudiments will certainly not ignore this tradition. But for the novice in the aesthetic domain this is hardly necessary, whereas perceiving some expressiveness is essential.

A second observation is that we can maintain without self-contradiction the views that (a) meanings are phenomenologically *in* the object and (b) we do not necessarily agree as to which meaning is being expressed by a given object at any given time. The reason for this lies in the multilayered meanings that sensory images can carry. The color red, for example, simultaneously conveys such meanings as courage, blood as the sustainer of

77

life, blood as the end of life, warmth in the physiological sense, warmth as the heat of passion, and the ideology of the Russian Communist party.

Suppose now that the color red appears in a painting or the word "red" is included in a line of poetry. Which of the many multiple associations will they tap? And how many of these will overlap and enfold each other? Of course, the context of the redness will limit the meanings evoked, but even then it would be rash to predict the response of any particular percipient. Whatever is expressed, however, by the principle of phenomenological objectivity will appear as being in the object, but it is quite conceivable that for Subject A meaning p is expressed by the object and to Subject B meaning r is expressed, and that both p and r are perceived as being in the same image.

Verdi's *Requiem* is just about as expressive a piece of music as I have ever heard, and I felt it to be so even before I compared the music with the text of the various parts of the mass. On the first hearing, the "Agnus Dei" sounded like the very essence of human sorrow and divine compassion. The music did not make me *think of* these qualities; it *sounded* sorrowful and compassionate. Yet if a critic were to report that he finds quite other qualities in the music, does it prove that what I heard I did not hear or that it was not there to be heard? And is it not possible that after reading the critic's account of his perception, I shall augment my own?

Susanne Langer has made us familiar with the truth that the "language of the arts" is not discursive, where each unit has a fixed meaning or set of meanings as set forth in the dictionary. On the contrary, the arts *present* us with images of feeling for which there is no dictionary save that of the totality of human experience. The more deeply we delve, the more likely we are to recognize a feeling in one of its infinite guises; there are no disguises.

One further consideration with regard to the difficulty of finding objective criteria for the expressive dimension of the aesthetic image deserves notice. Suppose, *mirabile dictu,* that one could assign definite meanings to bits of paint, notes, or gestures as we do to words. In other words, suppose we could have a dictionary of aesthetic symbols. A painting or a poem or a sonata would then be decipherable in the same way as a prose message, and works of art could then be means of unambiguous communication. Something vaguely resembling this is approximated in the ideographic symbols of such languages as Chinese. But for purposes of unambiguous communication, scientific mathematical language is a far more efficient tool than works of art. Indeed, if works of art were to serve solely as means of direct communication, there would be no art, or it would be displaced by science as fast as possible.

Without wishing to create paradoxes unnecessarily, it must be noted that indirect communication can on occasion be the most direct. Kierkegaard illustrates this by an odd example. Suppose, he asks, a man whom one has invited to dinner answers, "Yes, I'll be there, provided that a tile does not fall from a roof and kill me." As a direct communication this answer borders on foolishness. It is not even as sensible as the ritualistic caution "God willing," which is intoned in order to allay suspicion that one is taking too much for granted. So the communication, if it makes any sense at all, is indirect. Once we take it as such, the impact of the message is very powerful and direct, especially on one who, like Kierkegaard, is painfully aware of the confrontation between faith in God and faith in human reason.[2] All works of art are indirect communications, but to those who are sensitive to them they are direct and immediate.

Another difficulty in thinking of art as a form of direct or discursive communication is that art is supposed to be a product

[2] For further development of this theme, see Harry S. Broudy, "Kierkegaard on Indirect Communication," *Journal of Philosophy* 58 (1961): 226-233.

of the imagination. Now the glory of imagination is its unpredictability — therein lies its claim to creativity. An imagination
machine that turned out predictable creations would be a contra-
diction in terms. (Computers that turn out hitherto unthought-of
combinations are still not unpredictable and creative in the sense
that art claims to be.)

And yet I would not want to say that art is simply poor or
crude science, that we need art because we do not as yet know
how to predict every thought and feeling that men might have
under specified conditions. On the contrary, as Michael Polanyi,
Alfred North Whitehead, and others have observed, the work
of the scientist is also creative and imaginative. We cannot predict what a given scientist will find it important to investigate,
and although the formula he discovers may enable him to
predict events that hitherto had been unpredictable, that he
would become interested in finding this formula is not thereby
made more predictable. As Polanyi notes, a sense of the whole
reality to which a given inquiry may be pertinent is often a more
efficacious guide to the scientist's endeavors than the logic of the
field he is exploring: "The irreversible character of discovery
suggests that no solution of a problem can be accredited as a discovery if it is achieved by a procedure of following definite rules.
For such a procedure would be reversible in the sense that it
could be traced back stepwise to its beginning and repeated at
will any number of times, like any arithmetical computation. Accordingly any strictly formalized procedure would also be excluded as a means of achieving discovery."[3]

Kepler, for example, persisted with his hypothesis not because
of the evidence he had for it but in spite of the evidence against
it. It is this reference of science to deeper realms of feeling that
gives it vividness. This is not surprising, because events without
dramatic structure do not yield a "vivid sense of values," in

[3] Michael Polanyi, *Personal Knowledge* (Chicago: University of Chicago Press, 1958), p. 104.

Whitehead's terms. Science as finished is not a drama, but scientists are human and their scientific work is value-laden as all human activity is. The dramatic quality of scientific discovery is its aesthetic quality.

> A scientific theory which calls attention to its own beauty, and partly relies on it for claiming to represent empirical reality, is akin to a work of art which calls attention to its own beauty, as a token of artistic reality. It is akin also to the mystical contemplation of nature: a kinship shown historically in the Pythagorean origin of theoretical science. More generally, science, by virtue of its passionate note, finds its place among the great systems of utterances which try to evoke and impose correct modes of feeling. In teaching its own kinds of formal excellence science functions like art, religion, morality, law and other constituents of culture.[4]

For all of these reasons I am not unduly concerned with the paradox that the most important dimension of aesthetic experience is the least amenable to systematic instruction. This is not to say that one must remain silent about what a given work of art expresses. Students and teachers can utter their impressions to their hearts' content, but two safeguards should be insisted upon. One is that every judgment as to what a given item expresses should be referred to something in the work that can be perceived. If a student says that the seascape is that of an angry sea, then it is reasonable to ask what in the picture for him expresses this anger. The second condition is that there be no votes taken on what the class thinks a given work, or part of it, expresses.

The first precaution discourages pupils from using the work of art as a diving board for plunges into free association, which makes of art a pretext for nonaesthetic experience. The other precaution is necessary to inhibit premature and inauthentic interpretation. Given these precautions, interchange of opinions regarding expressiveness of what is being perceived can foster

[4] *Ibid.*, p. 133.

sensitivity to expressiveness. It does so by constantly reminding the percipient that works of art "talk" in metaphors, and inasmuch as the habit of looking for literal meanings where they are not to be found is one of the major obstacles to aesthetic competence, talk about expressiveness has its pedagogical merits.

I have not mentioned the technical aspects of the work of art. For one thing, the technical aspects have little to do with perceiving the import of the image, although they are important in constructing it. For another, many teachers who are sold on the notion that free experimentation is the proper approach to art education regard technical niceties as suitable for the professional artist, not the beginner. Premature concern with such technical matters, they think, inhibits the pupil from expressing himself. On the other side it can be argued that knowing how an aesthetic effect is produced does interest pupils, and when one undertakes to do art criticism or even to read much of it, discussion of techniques is important and, at any rate, unavoidable.

There is also the somewhat pedestrian psychological verity that admiration of skill is the first step toward genuine aesthetic appreciation. The zest and genuineness displayed in the appreciation of superior athletic performances are due in no small part to the circumstance that many of the spectators know how difficult it is to perform some of the feats they witness. The respect for skill is not an adequate substitute for aesthetic appreciation of the aesthetic image as such, but it is a pretty good introduction to it, and for this reason aesthetic educators might be well advised not to sell it short.

So much, then, for the general outline of the perceptual approach to aesthetic education; it is more modest than either the performance or the appreciation approach, and yet it is more fundamental than both. Given the habits of perceiving aesthetic images as do the painter, poet, dramatist, composer, choreographer, sculptor, and architect, authentic standards will be developed. Lacking these modes of perception, no amount of knowledge about the arts and no amount of allegiance to conventional standards will take its place.

There are, however, some other problems of aesthetic education that need strategic decisions, even if the perceptual approach is chosen. One of these is whether to teach the several arts separately or to combine them. I shall not rehearse the arguments in this controversy; I would rather rest the decision on the goal of aesthetic education in our culture and on the general economy of the school curriculum.

Inasmuch as there is little hope of the public school providing enough technical training in any one art to render the student a competent performer in it, and since general education should not preclude commerce with any of the arts, aesthetic education should cover as many of the arts as possible. The major objections to trying to cover more than one or two of the standard arts have to do with the fear of superficiality and the practical difficulties of recruiting an appropriate staff. The superficiality argument holds that it takes a long time to become proficient in any one art, so that if our pupils cannot become adept in even one art during the first twelve years of schooling, it is foolish to expect that they can become competent in a half dozen.

This objection is valid only if by proficiency we mean expertness in performance, but as will be indicated shortly, it does not necessarily hold against adequacy of perception. Given sufficient time and an acceptance of the perceptual approach, whether the arts are taught simultaneously or serially is of secondary importance. The unity of the approach and agreement on the dimensions of the aesthetic experience to be studied are a guarantee against haphazard fragmentation and capricious variations in emphasis.

The second objection is a serious one and in a way reflects the failure of our efforts in aesthetic education. Teachers who do arts education have been trained as monospecialists in music, literature, visual arts, dramatics, and often in some specialty within the broad fields. Nonspecialists do not regard themselves as competent to participate in aesthetic education at all, and monospecialists do not regard themselves as competent outside their specialty. As a result, whenever a program of aesthetic education is proposed, we tend to recruit a number of monospecialists who — if they believe in the idea at all — stipulate that they will not be called upon to step outside their special field of competence.

Since there is really no viable alternative to this mode of staffing — at least in our generation — it becomes necessary to find a captain of the team who is willing and able to talk with all the team members about their specialties. Furthermore, it is imperative that the team members be able to communicate with each other about their respective specialties. Without this minimum of communication, the course falls apart into performance or appreciation instruction in the separate arts, and this is where we came in. Now, granted the understandable reluctance of specialists to become generalists, why should their range of confidence be so limited? The very point we have been insisting upon is that as far as *perception* is concerned, all of us, even nonartists, should be able to perceive competently in all the major media.

At this point I shall ask the indulgence of the reader for some personal testimony to the effect that monospecialists in some arts, and even laymen, in a relatively short time can acquire the perceptual facility in media other than the ones in which they already are competent. In my own graduate seminar on aesthetic education at the University of Illinois the students, who come from the various arts, spend about one-third of the time on the key concepts of formal aesthetics and the remainder in demonstrating to the class how they perceive the aesthetic image (in its divers dimensions) in their own medium. Sometimes they use works of their own, at other times they may use familiar master-pieces; but in every instance they are expected to point to those features in the work that they regard as essential to perceive. They are to help us perceive as they perceive.

Each lesson takes the form of a descriptive analysis, a description of the sensory, formal, technical, and, to a lesser extent, expressive properties of the work under discussion. The class is not asked to like what the demonstrator likes or to concur in his judgment about the importance or significance of the work; often no such judgments are advanced. That might come in later courses, but in this seminar the immediate job is to get each member to detect the cues used by artists in the various media to "see" the picture or "hear" the music.

To the same end a rewarding experience was provided by Allen S. Weller, at that time dean of the University of Illinois College of Fine and Applied Arts. We asked Dean Weller to tell the seminar the factors he took into consideration when purchasing items (especially in contemporary painting) for the Krannert Museum. Perhaps the most important result of his discussion was the revelation of his way of perceiving contemporary painting. The cues or factors that he took into account were observable in the paintings which were being discussed, and the students of the seminar had no difficulty identifying them. And yet without his guidance the students might not have discerned them at all, a point which they themselves brought up repeatedly.

The seminar, I must admit, virtually taught itself, but it must be remembered that these were graduate students with a good deal of training in their own fields and often with teaching experience in those fields. Undergraduates, especially if they are not majors in one of the arts, would not be expected to give their own demonstrations, at least not right away: this task falls on the teacher or a team of teachers. Such a team will mess things up for everyone, however, unless there is agreement on the approach and some common understanding as to the concepts to be used in the descriptions and discussions. This explains the inclusion of formal aesthetics.

The same approach can be used not only in the training of teachers for aesthetic education but also for the teaching of aesthetic education to pupils in elementary and secondary schools (once the preliminary performance skills have been experimented with). Of course, one does not teach formal aesthetics *to* the pupils as such. Such study provides the conceptual framework *with* which the teacher teaches, but, like other frameworks, they are of special concern to the workman, not to the customer for whom he does the work. However, the demonstration by which teachers learn to perceive in many media is the method whereby pupils also learn to perceive.

One could, of course, spend much more than one semester on this sort of training in perception, but I am satisfied, as most of the students have been, that even in this short exposure, the combination of formal aesthetics and the demonstration lessons has made fairly clear to the participants just what "counts" for the painter, musicians, sculptor, choreographer, and architect. A colleague, Professor Ralph A. Smith, who is the founder and editor of the *Journal of Aesthetic Education,* reports similar experiences with his students.

The role of formal aesthetics perhaps needs a supplementary comment. First of all, it provides a vocabulary with which people in the various arts can discuss aesthetic materials. For example, the dimensions of the aesthetic image, the description of the aesthetic experience, the role of imagination, and the role of art in the social order are topics that are taken up in the formal study of aesthetics, as are theories of art and art criticism. The differentiation of aesthetic experience from other kinds and the possibility of objective norms for aesthetic judgments are also topics in aesthetics. Such a theoretical background is no substitute for direct experience with aesthetic objects, but it is a way of putting order into our discussions of that direct experience.

And when it comes to aesthetic education, there must be discussion, at least among those who are asked to make decisions on curriculum and teaching procedures. Thus in the seminar to which reference has been made, matters were facilitated enormously by the ability of the members to refer to the sensory, formal, technical, and expressive components of a work of art during the demonstration. Even more important, the study of aesthetics — scanty as it was — made the group wary of confusing descriptive analysis of a work of art with judgments about its artistic merits. "I like this work," "This work is good art," "This work has these properties" — assertions which at first were used almost interchangeably — were carefully distinguished by the end of the seminar. Finally, the class became sensitive to the difference between what was to be perceived in the work and the theories that explained or tried to explain why the artist did what he did, on the one hand, and why we responded to the work as we did (or were supposed to), on the other hand.

Verbal quibbling? Perhaps some of the distinctions were overfinely drawn; perhaps, on occasion, the theory drifted too far from the concrete works of nature and artists. But most of the diffidence people feel about art, especially serious art, results from the way they believe they ought to *think* and *talk* about it rather than from what they perceive. Accordingly, aesthetic education, in at least one sense, means getting the young to think and speak properly about art, so that their cognition does not distort their perception.

The results of these seminars and similar ventures have some bearing on the preparation of teachers of aesthetic education courses (or some variants of the humanities courses that involve the related arts).

In the perceptual approach the most feasible design for teacher preparation is something like this:

1. Recruit monospecialists in the arts.

2. Have them enroll in at least one course in formal aesthetics.

3. Have them enroll in at least one seminar or course, but preferably two, in aesthetic education using the perceptual approach as outlined above.

4. Have them enroll in at least one, and possibly two, workshops on methods and materials from the various arts.

This course work, supplemented by practice teaching in aesthetic education programs already in force, should enable teachers to head up or participate in a team effort in organizing and providing instruction at the secondary level. Of course, the same form of preparation could work equally well at the elementary level, where team teaching is applicable. A similar type of preparation could be adapted for the general elementary classroom teacher, except that one probably would not recruit monospecialists in step 1 above. I see no reason, however, for not adapting and supplementing the work in music and art that is now part of the teacher training program for elementary teachers so that it serves as preparation for aesthetic education. Of course, as time goes by and the general education of all teachers already includes sound work in aesthetic education, this type of training will become more feasible.

At a number of colleges of education and teachers' colleges efforts are being made to design programs of teacher preparation for some form of aesthetic education. (The Central Midwestern Regional Educational Laboratory is also interested in this type of education and is producing materials appropriate to it.) The materials developed by the Education Research Council of America, with headquarters in Cleveland, exemplify a program that has been used very successfully in the elementary grades with the perceptual approach. There is no dearth of materials for aesthetic education, but there is a dearth of confidence that anyone but a specialist in one of the arts can perceive aesthetically in a given art. This skepticism I believe is unwarranted.

I have undertaken this long digression in order to present some evidence for the view that aesthetic education as perception is not so mysterious a branch of pedagogy as some people believe, for either the teacher or the pupil. While some experience with performance helps matters considerably, neither the pupil nor the teacher needs artistic talent to learn to perceive properly. Furthermore, the results — changes in perception — came fairly quickly, quickly enough to sustain the efforts of the learners.

In closing this section of the discussion, I want to agree with the specialists that each art has its own mode of experience, which is not to be confused with or substituted for by experience with another art. Form in painting, for example, is not the same experience as form in poetry or drama, but all art works have form, and pedagogically it is important that we perceive form in each art as the specialists do. I would differ from the views of some specialists, however, that only by becoming a performing specialist can one perceive in the manner of the specialist. This I think to be false.

V

The Problem of Standards in Aesthetic Education

THE approach to aesthetic education through the training of perception may quiet the fear of the liberationists that the school will impose conventional or "establishment" standards of taste and art on the defenseless pupil. But this very assurance of interpretive neutrality is viewed with dismay — by those who favor aesthetic education as a means of inculcating the positive values of classical humanism, the Judeo-Christian tradition, the old-line liberalism of Franklin Delano Roosevelt's day, or the low-key liberalism of dissident Republicans of our own times. I exclude the John Birchers and the counter-culturists because they function mainly as harassers of the middle groups, who seriously and intelligently regard schooling as an important avenue to value education.

It is unavoidable, therefore, that the problem of standards in aesthetic experience be met directly; otherwise, aesthetic education will continue to flourish or languish, as the case may be, as an elective frill to be eliminated in times of financial retrenchment. Or it may be taken seriously and become an ideological football, as one group or another becomes the dominant force in the community. The latter possibility is especially dangerous at a time when no common value commitment obtains in the community.

The problem is exacerbated by the widespread acceptance of two diametrically opposed views. One is that in art, as in everything else, there is a difference between good and bad, that this difference is readily ascertainable, and that the school ought to be on the side of the good — unequivocally. In this view teachers who disagree with what is "generally accepted" as good in all realms of value, and in the arts as well, should be invited to leave the system — and possibly the country as well. This outlook is vigorously stated in the newspapers every time a school library stocks books which, on the accepted view, are immoral or pornographic or revolutionary in one sense or another. A painting or mural in the school building having the alleged harmful properties likewise embroils the community and the school authorities. I think this view — and the harassers on both extremes exploit it — is an unfortunate one and ought to be resisted by the school at every turn, but on what grounds can it justify its resistance?

The opposite view is that in values, especially in the aesthetic ones, all judgments are really confessions of taste, and about taste rational men do not dispute. Hence any curriculum in aesthetic education will either indoctrinate arbitrarily or must abjure value judgments entirely. About half of the grounds for this view lie in a belief that value judgments are not about observable states of affairs but, rather, are the results of individual histories; they are idiosyncratic, relative to the culture or the individual, and cannot be universalized. On this view "This is a good painting" can mean no more than "I like this painting" or "People in this culture like this painting." On either interpretation one important assumption for education is excluded, viz., "The pupil ought to like or approve this painting." Instead we are told that cultural pluralism is the only viable stance in a culture such as ours. This pluralism has been stressed in recent years because ethnic minorities have rejected the melting-pot notion that was so popular in our country during the first half of the twentieth century. The melting-pot idea did not deny ethnic differences, but it did deny that they were really important — interesting yes, important no. The important values — democracy, freedom to advance economically, schooling as a means of social mobility — were supposed to be shared by all.

The social unrest among ethnic minorities and in the counterculture of the last decade impugns the desirability of these common values because they are accessible only to the members of the dominant white middle class and therefore not a valid criterion for all other classes. It is this doubt that has rendered the public schools vulnerable to attacks from all sides and gives superficial credence to the charge that they have failed. If success means that all segments of our population have achieved the virtues and blessings of middle-class whites, then, of course, they have failed, as have all of our social institutions.

And yet if formal schooling gives up the right to direct its work by norms, on what grounds can it justify instruction at all? And if it is forced to direct its work by a multiplicity of incompatible norms, is instruction even possible? The continued existence of the public schools in our country depends on their being able to invoke norms for instruction that transcend ethnic and social differences. Otherwise we shall gravitate toward a multiplicity of schools, each designed to carry out the value commitments of this or that group. Who can say how many such groups will emerge?

The other half of the difficulty with norms in aesthetic education lies in the belief that the response to the aesthetic object is made up of associations aroused in the viewer's mind. "The Star-Spangled Banner" arouses sentiments of patriotism, a placid landscape arouses youthful memories of romantic episodes, *Guernica* reinstates memories of war and destruction. The response aroused by a given painting, drama, or poem would thus depend almost entirely on the associations peculiar to the individual; therefore, whether a work of art is good, bad, or indifferent is a highly individual and even personal matter. How can such judgments be true or false?

If the school were to take these arguments seriously — and in the field of the arts it is more likely to do so than in other value areas — then really only one course is open to it. It is to expose the pupil to the widest variety of aesthetic stimuli and let nature take its course. The free experimental approach, about which much is written, does try to do something like this. The pupil is urged to do and undergo whatever he pleases with whatever art materials the school can provide; talk of standards is belligerently silenced. The pupil is allowed to express how he *feels* about his own work, and he alone decides whether it needs improvement and what improvement shall mean.

The difficulty with taking this permissive stance seriously is that it is almost impossible to be true to it in any strict sense. The moment the school chooses some materials and not others, it is executing an implicit value judgment; indeed, its lack of commitment to objective standards is itself a commitment of the greatest significance.

If exposure to the widest variety of aesthetic experiences is to be the approach to aesthetic education, then the school is not in a good position to do even a fair job of it. For one thing, the school can never expose the pupil to more than a tiny fraction of aesthetic objects. It cannot match the resources of museums, libraries, and the great musical organizations as far as serious art is concerned; nor can it compete with the mass media as regards resources of popular art. At most, schools can try to bring very selected samples of art to pupils located in remote rural areas or backward regions. Even these could be reached more efficiently by television than by the meager resources that schools can muster. The school, therefore, cannot avoid being selective in the materials it chooses for instruction. The moment it begins selecting, the pose of value neutrality collapses, and the school lays itself open to the charge of indoctrination under the guise of nonindoctrination.

Those of us who are committed to the importance of aesthetic education cannot dodge the problem of standards, but it is essential that we make as clear as we can to the school-board members, school administrators, teachers, and parents just what sort of standards we can or cannot support. Steering a middle course between absolute standards and no standards is a futile strategy. For if a standard means anything, there is a point beyond which it stops being flexible and becomes nonnegotiable. Nevertheless, what can or cannot be negotiated can vary. In other words, to operate as instructional agencies, schools must have a criterion of what at any given time must be taken as nonnegotiable, as given. Beyond these limits presumably lie the negotiable areas. It is to the delimitations of these areas and the claims that may grow out of them that I would like now to address myself.

AESTHETIC AND NONAESTHETIC VALUE NORMS

We are concerned with two sorts of norms in aesthetic education: one has to do with what is good and bad, right and wrong, important and unimportant in life as a whole (extra-aesthetic norms); the other has to do with what is aesthetically or artistically good. If aesthetic education is urged by the school as an avenue to value education in general, then the public has a right to ask what effect aesthetic education will have on standards of conduct in general. In addition, the public has a right to know whether the program will form in the pupil a commitment to "good" art rather than to some other kind.

What, then, should the role of aesthetic education be for nonaesthetic values?

Feelings influence value commitments and therefore choice and action. Hence the quality of behavior in the home and the community could be influenced by images, possibly by those images we have called aesthetic. The influence can be fairly direct, as in television programs that in the form of fiction or advertising make one type of behavior more or less attractive than another. If youthful insouciance is celebrated on one television program after another, then one can assume that the viewers will form values in this direction. Whatever a culture celebrates in its arts is taken as an index of importance. For this reason totalitarian countries keep close tabs on what their artists are up to. Clearly ours is not, and one would hope never will be, a totalitarian country, and therefore selecting art to promote directly this or that set of official values is out of the question for the culture or the school. But is there an unofficial set of values that the community accepts and that therefore should be respected by the school in its aesthetic education?

This view must also be rejected, for whether the community's value preferences are official or unofficial is beside the point. The heart of the matter lies in the "right" or the authority of the school in the matter of values. Where does it get authority for its value judgments? In a democratic society the ultimate political authority is the will of the people, usually determined by a vote. It is natural in such a society to speak of the schools as "belonging to the people" and to assert that the people must have the final decision on what goes on in them. The argument is irrefutable if by authority we mean political authority, i.e., authority to act in the name of the people. Even here it is only when a society agrees to act as if the will of the majority were the will of the totality — which it almost never is — that it makes sense to say that *vox populi* is *vox dei*. But the authority we are talking about is not to decide what shall be *done* in the name of the body politic but, rather, on how to arrive at judgments of truth and falsity, good and evil, aesthetic value and disvalue. We are not trying to determine a course of collective action but, instead, to ascertain the grounds for the validity of judgment in the various domains of value.

Charles Sanders Peirce defined truth as the opinion fated to be ultimately agreed upon by all who investigate: "Truth is that concordance of an abstract statement with the ideal limit towards which endless investigation would tend to bring scientific belief. . . ."[1] Truth in all realms for practical purposes depends on agreement, but whereas in the political realm it is the agreement of all the voters, in the realm of knowledge it is the agreement of those who investigate. For this reason we do not hold elections to decide what shall be taught in biology, chemistry, history, literature, and the other fields of instruction. The Scopes trial, one might hope, marked the demise of the view that we should.

On what grounds do we reject the criterion of *vox populi* in chemistry, biology, economics, history, and the other intellectual disciplines that make up the curriculum? Furthermore, to what authority do we appeal when a segment of the community objects to what is being taught in these disciplines? We appeal to the authority of the discipline itself, and where is that authority lodged? It is lodged in the experts who carry on investigations in that discipline, the credentialed members of that discipline. Who are the credentialed members? Those who have qualified by receiving instruction from credentialed members and whose performance has been approved by their credentialed peers. Over the centuries one credentialing group after another has been initiating new members. At any given time the canons of inquiry are accepted by the credentialing group, and thus although each decade may witness some changes in the criteria of what is good chemistry or biology or economics, at no time do the individual members of the credentialing group claim that there are no standards or that one standard is as acceptable as another.

The continuity of the credentialing group constitutes what may be called the community or the consensus of the learned as to

[1] *The Collected Papers of Charles Sanders Peirce,* ed. C. Hartshorne, P. Weiss, and A. W. Burks (Cambridge, Mass.: Harvard University Press, 1931-1958), 5: 565.

what is important and true in a given field of inquiry. All developments emerge from this consensus, and whether or not a new discovery is long- or short-lived depends on acceptance by the credentialing group. "Thus we may regard, in the last analysis, the entire superior knowledge embodied in a modern highly articulate culture as the sum total of what its classics have uttered and its heroes and saints have done."[2]

Two points cannot be overemphasized in this account of the authority of the learned. One is that this authority is accepted on faith by the credentialing group. Each member does not repeat the discoveries by virtue of which the tradition was built up. Second, this authority does not necessarily impede new discoveries, although it may delay the acceptance of them. The new discoveries are the work of the more imaginative and talented spirits *within* the discipline who go beyond the accepted views and theories, but not before they have been inducted into the tradition.

Traditionalism, Polanyi points out, is based on the notion that we are required to believe before we can know, and this is grounded in the theory that discovery is guided and sustained by a conviction (a belief) that there is a hidden reality to be found and understood. This belief presumably is precisely what the tradition supplies to the school and indeed to every systematic thinker and doer.

> The popular conception of science teaches that science is a collection of observable facts, which anybody can verify for himself. We have seen that this is not true in the case of expert knowledge, as in diagnosing a disease. But it is not true either in the physical sciences. In the first place, you cannot possibly get hold of the equipment for testing, for example, a statement of astronomy or of chemistry. And supposing you could somehow get the use of an observatory or a chemical laboratory, you would probably damage their instruments beyond repair before you ever made an observa-

[2] Polanyi, *Personal Knowledge,* p. 376.

tion. And even if you should succeed in carrying out an observation to check up on a statement of science and you
found a result which contradicted it, you would rightly assume that you had made a mistake.

The acceptance of scientific statements by laymen is based
on authority, and this is true to nearly the same extent for
scientists using results from branches of science other than
their own. Scientists must rely heavily for their facts on the
authority of fellow scientists.[3]

Under these circumstances a school can defend its decisions
by appeal to the learned tradition and the credentialing authorities of the disciplines. To be sure, politically this does not settle
the matter. A board could be elected that would defy the learned
tradition, and at that point all teachers and administrators would
be faced by a moral dilemma — either acquiesce in the board's
decision and betray the learned tradition, or accept the tradition
and forfeit their jobs. Politically it should not be necessary for the
individual teacher or administrator to face this dilemma alone,
and he would not if the school establishment gave undivided
allegiance to the learned tradition in all the domains of its activities. This, I believe, the teaching profession and indeed the
whole educational establishment must do. May I repeat that this
allegiance does not prevent a diversity of views within the discipline, but it does preclude the nonexpert from claiming the right
to join in the controversy. Every man has a right to his own views
on anything, in the sense that nobody can prevent his having
them, but for his view to be authoritative, it has to be the result
of inquiry approved by the canons of the relevant discipline.

Before going on with the discussion of the authority of the
learned tradition in the realm of aesthetic value, it may be advis-
able to raise the possibility that aesthetic values affect the choice
patterns of men in a less direct way than has been discussed. An
advertisement featuring a lithe young woman leaping in the

[3] Michael Polanyi, *The Tacit Dimension* (New York: Doubleday, 1966), pp. 63-64.

ocean waves and singing a paean for a soft drink is a direct appeal to the viewer to imagine herself with the attributes of the young woman, which are presumably obtainable by buying large quantities of the soft drink. But even here there is an indirect influence of the image, or at least there can be. If, for example, the pleasing aspects of the visual image are actually perceived as being in the beverage, i.e., if the beverage is perceived as having the exuberant vitality of the young lady in the image, then a bottle of the stuff has itself taken on an aesthetic quality. It has become expressive by a metaphor which presents us with the news that the beverage tastes as the girl looks — alive, vibrant, desirable. Automobiles, furs, and houses can "look" expensive or exclusive or respectable, and when this appearance is achieved, an aesthetic image has been created. In perceiving this image, we contemplate richness, exclusiveness, and social solidity not in their ordinary habitats but as visual forms. We thus come to understand these feeling qualities, and this may or may not be accompanied by a desire to go out and purchase the car and furs.

Thus aesthetic perception may influence value and choice very indirectly, and while the more direct influence will appeal more potently to the layman interested in the defense and promotion of the conventional values, we should hesitate to promise too much direct help of this sort in aesthetic education. Perhaps the matter could be put more concretely by the following example.

In our culture weddings are closely tied to a legal-religious ritual. The Christian version involves such symbols as veils, rings, prayers, incantations, and the exchange of vows. The ceremony may be embellished by music, flowers, costumes, and decorations. Sometimes the ceremony is held in the open in surroundings designed to give natural beauty to the occasion. Do such rituals and their aesthetic accompaniments add anything to the social and individual significance of marriage? From the rebellious young one gets a resounding "no" for an answer. Indeed, the rejection of conventional rituals is regarded as the first step toward liberation from the social restrictions of the establishment, and a formal conventional wedding is looked upon as something contrived by parents, flower merchants, and caterers, not to say clergymen. The "real" marriage, they would argue, is the love relation between the partners, and with this the legal, religious, and social rituals have nothing to do.

Of course, this is not even half true. Love and marriage do not go together like a horse and carriage. In many cultures the romantic love relation has little to do with marriage, and even in our own culture the law does not recognize romantic love as a necessary or sufficient cause of either marriage or divorce. Marriage is a covenant entered into for the purposes of companionship and sexual gratification, to be sure, but, as far as the state is concerned, primarily for the purpose of establishing an establishment called the family. Hence the marriage event is the concern not merely of the couple to be married but of the whole community. When the extended family was still in vogue, it was very important for the couple to adjust to a wide assortment of in-laws and relatives. The modern nuclear family reduces the need for adjustment considerably. The law notes the union and makes certain regulations applicable to it. The marriage ceremony serves notice of a new set of relationships to be observed not only by the couple but by others in the community. For example, neither partner is now eligible for courtship, and both surrender some freedom of movement and action hitherto accorded them.

The wedding ceremony is supposed to ritualize all of these new events and their implications. The church, the law, the parents, the relatives, the citizens — all are in on the act and affirm the importance of the occasion. Symbolism and solemnity, joyousness and a sly salaciousness, romantic bliss and vows of eternal fidelity, youthful ardor and thoughts of parental responsibility, a new independence and a new dependence — all of these and many, many more feelings are to be conveyed, imaged, and objectified by the ceremony. The aesthetic dimensions of the ritual bear most of this burden; the total situation must be pervaded by the feeling tones appropriate to the occasion. This is achieved by the creation of appropriate aesthetic images.

In a fairly stable culture these rituals remain constant over long periods, so that each generation perceives them as invitations to respond with the appropriate emotions. Funerals, christenings, national victories, and holidays all use aesthetic means to ritualize and objectify the emotions these occasions are intended to elicit and reinforce. So used, art is an instrument for reinforcing certain social emphases; it is a socializing force. When a culture fails to ritualize its red-letter days, social control and community of feeling are that much harder to secure and maintain. Rituals are usually not contrived, at least not those that survive for very long. Invented rituals always strike us as being silly. Unless the occasion to be ritualized is important and vivid enough to stir the imagination of sensitive members of the group, no ritual is likely to develop. Conversely, if the event is "memorable," its essential imagery will stir the imagination of the artist to drama and song, and this image will become the substitute for the original experience, almost as a caricature takes the place of a photograph of a face.

Even more indirectly, aesthetic education will affect the valuational structure of the individual and the community through the refinement of perception and the broadening volume of feeling potential. By and large, this latter indirect effect is more important than the direct reinforcement of extra-aesthetic values, although it is somewhat more difficult to "sell" than the direct one. Why a more developed aesthetic sensitivity is a social asset and why individuals should be encouraged to cultivate it demand a justification that brings us back to the problem of standards and the authority of the school to "impose" such norms on pupils who are not in a position to resist.

Reference has been made to consensus of the learned as the principle of authority to which the school can appeal when confronted with political pressures. In the arts this principle is promulgated in at least two ways: by the quasi-official body of critics who pass judgment on current works and by the learned tradition, which is the crystallized residue of the judgments of generations of critics on the art of the past.

In most fields of intellectual endeavor the legitimacy of the learned tradition is now taken for granted. As Thomas Kuhn has noted, the induction of new workers into a scientific field is through "paradigm science," by which he means that well-defined set of problems or puzzles on which most of the working members of the guild are employed.[4] Revolutionary science, that which is fermenting at the frontier of the discipline, is reserved for the creative workers who may under certain circumstances force a revision of the paradigms themselves and thus lay the groundwork for new paradigms.

Almost the exact opposite of this situation obtains in the arts and in aesthetic education. Here the unspoiled spontaneity of childhood and the uninhibited ignorance of the tyro are more highly regarded than trained maturity. Indeed, some commentators have made the point that counter-culture art deliberately downgrades art made by experts for appreciation by an inexpert audience. Instead, the audience is invited to participate in creating the art object itself — whether it be a play, a dance, a piece of music, a wall painting, or a film — no special expertise is necessary.

Similarly, the critical tradition in the arts is held suspect; it is regarded as the dead hand of the past that stifles the creativity of the child and the unspoiled beginner. But is the case in the arts so much different from that in the sciences? I think not. In the realm of values in general, and in that of aesthetic values in particular, we have to look, listen, and feel, with forms of feeling that are learned just as the categories of science are

[4] Thomas Kuhn, *The Structure of Scientific Revolutions* (Chicago: University of Chicago Press, 1962), p. 11.

learned. We are no more and no less original and spontaneous in the realm of the arts than we are in any other department of our culture.

However, there are many grades of participation. They range from the use of simple, milieu-conditioned norms at one end to highly cultivated norms at the other. The problem of standards in art, as far as education is concerned, is solved in the same way as it is solved in other fields of instruction. For the induction of the young the judgment of the experts, the connoisseurs — whether in their consensus or disagreement — is the only viable criterion. Authenticity of standards consists not in their originality or uniqueness. They are not authentic *simply* because they are mine but, rather, because I accept and introject them via the same sort of perception, analysis, and reflection as is used by the experts. Moreover, the objectivity of the aesthetic judgment lies not in the overwhelming agreement among the judges but, rather, in their agreement as to what in a work of art shall count as relevant evidence for such judgments.

I hope that these remarks on the problem of standards will serve to restore some confidence to those who are engaged in aesthetic education or who are trying to promote it in the schools. To the objection that we do not know what good and bad, better and worse, mean in the aesthetic domain, we can retort that they mean no more and no less than they mean in any other field of instruction which boasts a critical tradition nurtured by a professional guild. As to the objection that even if we did know what good and bad or better and worse meant, we would have no right to impose such judgments on the innocent young, we can remind the objector that we live by validated authority in every area of our lives and education. Imposition is not bad in itself, only when it cannot be justified by the authority of the intellect itself.

VI

Why Enlightened Cherishing?

G RANTED that what has been said about standards makes some sense, what implications does it have for aesthetic education?

1. The adoption of the suggested criteria enables us to defend the mode of perception used by practitioners of the various arts as the right ones, the ones we would like to foster in our pupils.

2. When we go beyond perception to judgment and cherishing, the critical tradition provides us with exemplars in each art that are worth our extended study. For each exemplar there is a rationale that justifies our paying attention to it. It may, like a play of Shakespeare, be the work of a genius that explores experience over a great range and creates aesthetic images that remain interesting to perception over the centuries. A work may summarize a whole period, as does the *Divine Comedy* of Dante. Or it may display characteristics that presage later movements, e.g., the novels of Melville, the poetry of Eliot, the painting of Hieronymus Bosch, Goya, and Cézanne. Or it may express with unusual power or clarity the spirit of an age, e.g., the poetry of Homer or the painting of the Middle Ages.

There is an important sense in which the whole critical tradition needs to be understood and felt in order to approach the frontier of contemporary art. Artists may be trying to express the world as they see it, but most of the time they see the world through the eyes of their fellow artists past and present. The great body of art scholarship, history, criticism, and treatises on style and form constitute the knowledge and lore of mankind's aesthetic adventures, just as the museums and libraries contain the surviving works of art which inspired the scholarship in the first place. Anyone who makes any pretense of being cultivated in the arts will become familiar, of course, with the salient items of both the works of art and the scholarship about them. Whether during or after each study one adopts the criteria of the tradition, selects from among them, or rejects them altogether, it will be an educated choice.

T. S. Eliot said about the critic, "So the critic to whom I am most grateful is the one who can make me look at something I have never looked at before, or looked at only with eyes clouded with prejudice, set me face to face with it and then leave me alone with it. From that point, I must rely upon my own sensibility, intelligence, and capacity for wisdom."[1] This is fine for T. S. Eliot, who already had well-developed sensibility, intelligence, and capacity for wisdom, precisely that which the pupil does not yet have. Eliot, one must suppose, had already introjected models that guided his aesthetic judgments. To what extent Eliot developed his own models I do not know, but one can safely wager that however much they were his own, they were modifications of standards that were developed from models espoused by critics from Aristotle on.

Two important objections can and often do arise at this juncture. One is: Why should we bother to become cultivated? Why should cherishing be enlightened? The second kind of question is related to the first; it asks: Why cannot we be satisfied with the popular arts, those that do not require study? Must we go into serious art, the kind that art historians write about?

[1] T. S. Eliot, *On Poetry and Poets* (London: Faber and Faber, 1957), p. 117, quoted by Jerome Stolnitz in *Aesthetics and Philosophy of Art Criticism* (Boston: Houghton Mifflin, 1960).

Consider, for example, the following question: Is it desirable and necessary to teach English to all our citizens? Everyone who has had to read college compositions and who has cringed at the linguistic stumbling of some of our elected officials would say "yes" vehemently. Yet for all practical purposes, syntactical sloppiness does not hamper communication or even expression — if one accepts evidence from modern novels. For ordinary discourse sloppy English usage must be judged as adequate. In their occupational life people speak a special jargon with as much technical precision as the situation demands. So why urge more and better English instruction? The hidden premise is that something called "educated English" is better than the English most people, young and old, do in fact use. This premise need only be challenged in theory[2] — as it is ignored in practice — and the cry for more and better English instruction becomes a hollow echo of snobbery.

An embarrassing parallel is found in aesthetic education. That human beings have aesthetic experience and that they do not live, and probably cannot live, without art need no elaborate proof. However, the art they most often choose to live with is plentiful and easily available, and it does for them just about what they want it to do. Popular music celebrates love, conflict, yearning, and victory. Young people thrill to it; older ones dream by it. If everything is fine and everyone is happy with his aesthetic state, why the push for more and better music education? Do we have here also a hidden premise? Do we secretly believe that "good" music or "serious" music or "classical" music is better than popular music and that everyone should enjoy it or at least help to support it? I say "secretly" advisedly, because openly the philosophers vie with one another in challenging us to distinguish between good and bad music, serious and popular music. And what theoreticians do by technical argument, teenagers accomplish with scornful hoots in the argot of the day.

Cultivation has the connotation of deliberate and directed in-

[2] As did the builders of the most recent Webster's dictionary.

tervention. In cultivating a garden, one intervenes to destroy weeds and to increase the nitrogen content of the soil. Pruning, watering, and hoeing are all interventions; they utilize natural processes, but they produce what otherwise might not have been. Cultivation is the opposite of letting matters alone — to develop according to some given set of inner determinants or chance. Formal schooling is a prime example of cultivation.

But should the school intervene in the aesthetic life of the pupil, and if so on what grounds? It seems to me that there are a number of arguments on which one might rest the case for such cultivation:

1. The argument from the connoisseur.

2. The argument from the different roles of serious and popular art as regards projection of new life styles.

3. The more general argument for the breadth and precision that systematic study and reflection produce in the development of the individual.

4. The argument that cultivation can only go so far without some help from formal tuition.

The simplest argument for cultivation, whether it is of English usage or the collection of antique automobiles, is the satisfaction of those who become connoisseurs or, more colloquially, buffs in any field. The process of becoming a buff begins with some special impetus; it may be that one's neighbor is collecting antique automobiles, or one is inherited from an eccentric uncle. So adventitious is the cause of the special interest that we almost always ask a buff why in the world he chose to become one. In other words, it is virtually impossible to predict who will become an avid collector of teacups, Indian arrows, or histories of families named Robinson. Since one's life work, if freely chosen, is also a form of "buffism," the same unpredictability applies to a choice of vocation.

Once the special interest is implanted, sensitivity to differences in the phenomena of the chosen field develops. To the uninitiated in baseball, for example, all batters look about alike and swing alike. Not so to the buff. To him every major-league batter has his own stance and characteristic mannerisms at the plate. This differentiation continues until the tiniest differences become significant. The connoisseur is the person to whom small differences make a big difference.

Concomitantly with the proliferation of fine distinctions comes awareness of ever more widely ranging similarities, and on these similarities generalizations are built: "All Chinese pottery of a certain dynasty has characteristics A, B, and C," "All Madonnas of a certain period are painted with blue robes," "All mushrooms of a certain sort are poisonous."

At this point the buff, the connoisseur, the expert, the scholar — call him what you will — becomes a bore to the layman. The layman, unless he has some special need for the objects in which the connoisseur is engrossed, is not interested in their minute peculiarities. If he is not interested in collecting antique automobiles, what does he care about the differences between the construction of one old Ford and another? Or if he goes to a ball game once or twice a year to edify his young sons, why should he be enchanted with disquisitions on the differences in the batting stances of a score or so of batters who are paraded before him? Boring as the connoisseur is to the layman, the layman is an even greater trial to the buff, but his eyes light up when he encounters a fellow connoisseur. Buffs tend to congregate and form organizations to exchange information but especially to acquire conversational partners. Thus is born the cult of the cultivated.

If one now asks the buff why he is a buff, he will reply in one of two ways: "It gives me a great deal of satisfaction; it interests me," or "If you have to ask me why I am a buff, you won't understand any explanation I try to give you." Of the two answers the latter is the more instructive because he to whom fine distinctions make little difference can never understand somebody to whom minute differences make so much difference. Connoisseurship is satisfying because the connoisseur has stimulated his intellectual powers in making new discriminations and syntheses. That is what being intellectual means. Most of what is called scholarship consists of putting asunder concepts other men have joined and joining ideas others have differentiated. Furthermore, the buff is on a quest that has no end; it gives his life a purpose, a perpetual drive, for the true buff is always straining to get a top-flight specimen of his specialty. Finally, there is the internal steadfastness, almost serenity, that comes from knowing what is really first-rate in a domain. In a life full of uncertainty, in which one must depend on the judgments of others in so many affairs, to be one's own judge is at once both an exhilarating and a steadying influence.

Perhaps the satisfaction that comes from cultivation is best brought out by asking a buff whether he could return to his pre-buff tastes. Can the gourmet be satisfied with rough, catch-as-catch-can cookery? Once in a while he can, but even then only because some types of simple cookery create flavors that are themselves distinctive. It is difficult to enjoy less than the best once one has learned to love the best. Cultivation can spoil us for lesser goods. In a world where the higher goods are limited, cultivation may bring discontent. That is why if connoisseurship is taken as a way of life, one must choose fields in which the satisfactions do not rely too much on external goods and the vagaries of fortune. Fortunately, in the intellectual, moral, and aesthetic domains connoisseurship requires relatively few hostages to fortune. Indeed, the more one's own resources in these areas are cultivated, the less does one have to rely on money, people, or good fortune.

Unfortunately, cultivation is not confined to positive values. One can cultivate a taste for sadism, for selfishness, for despotic power. Unless we specify the goals for which one is being cultivated, we are in no position to pass judgment on the enterprise. Thus although adequate perception is the basic ability to be fostered in aesthetic education, enlightened cherishing goes beyond the perception of the aesthetic image as such. It is to the cultural heritage that we must turn for the goals of cultivation as well as the process. This heritage has preserved many styles of the good life and the judgments of men and history upon them. The heritage has models for imitation and the apparatus for the criticism of them.

The buff phenomenon is an example of how systematic cultivation of a field through study and reflection contributes to the breadth of our interests and the precision of our thinking. Naturally this would also be the case with cultivation in the forms of feeling which aesthetic images objectify, and this brings us to the argument concerning serious and popular art.

SERIOUS AND POPULAR ART

It is difficult to draw a distinction between serious art and popular art. Certainly popular art is art that has a wide appeal, and serious art can be characterized as being created for the sake of aesthetic value, but this does not give us mutually exclusive classes. Some very popular operatic arias would also have to be called serious art, and some music designed for entertainment may show high artistic merit. Nor can we speak of serious art as that which only a few people like, because some art intended to be popular does not hit the jackpot and fails to captivate the multitude. Sometimes the term "serious art" is reserved for works that are expressions of the artist's outlook on life, but it is hard to deny that some very popular works also serve this purpose.

However, for our purpose the distinction can be made out with reasonable clarity. Serious art in any medium is art that is taken seriously as art, and this means that there exists a set of persons, artists, critics, performers, and scholars who select it for their study and connoisseurship. The objects they select as deserving of study as art are serious art, regardless of the intent of the artist or the acceptance by the general public. Thus if jazz is taken seriously as an art form, and there is a body of buffs and scholarship about jazz, then certain composers of jazz music, who are part of the buff group, are serious artists.

In this view popular art means (a) art that is widely accepted and (b) art that requires no connoisseurship or special training for its appreciation. In other words, popular art is consumed, appreciated, and enjoyed, but it is not studied. If one should undertake the study of such art, then of course one would have become serious about it, but such study is a field of connoisseurship and as such not popular in the sense the original was. Does study make popular art serious? There is no lack of sociological inquiry into popular music, fiction, and movies: does this qualify these objects as serious art?

Here one must enter a reservation. To take something seriously and for something to be capable of sustaining a serious interest are not the same thing. If an object or a field of objects is not rich to begin with, there is little reward for drawing fine distinctions and making new syntheses. There is only just so much that one can do with singing commercials, for example, or with a score of popular songs in any given season. Serious art, in addition to being taken seriously by connoisseurs, tends to be complex; it tends to engage life at its deeper levels. In gaining wide appeal, popular art cannot cater to esoteric tastes and overly discriminating judgments (although there may be exceptions), just as manufacturers of ready-made clothes cannot cater to unusual body types and tastes. In popular art emotions must be expressed in broad, easily recognizable images; the idiom in which they are expressed must be familiar; and deviations from the stereotype in both content and form must be quite small. For this reason the popular arts or popular art is conservative; it expresses value commitments the public has already made. Hence nothing dates a period so readily as its popular music, drama, and fiction.

Serious art, on the other hand, is esoteric in two ways. In its classic forms, i.e., the forms preserved and praised by critical tradition, it appeals only to a small, cultivated public, to those who have become familiar with that tradition. In its avant-garde state it is highly experimental in form, content, or both and alienates not only the general public but often the critical public as well. Thus it is a common complaint that the major symphony orchestras in the United States prefer to stick with the old favorites and are reluctant to present experimental compositions. In this they are reflecting the tastes of their patrons, usually the cultural elite of the community.

Avant-garde art, therefore, like revolutionary or frontier science, requires a special public to sustain it in the face of general animosity. The critical tradition, realizing that in its history avant-garde "monstrosities" often became the classics of a later generation, e.g., Stravinsky's *Rite of Spring* or many of the works of Picasso, is wary of rejecting the plethora of avant-garde experiments as rubbish because they do not meet criteria of the classic art or the art of the academy. Who is willing to predict, for example, how much of pop art, op art, constructionism, aleatory music, and a score of other innovations will survive the century? Yet impressionism and cubism, which once disconcerted the critics no less than do some of the wild goings-on of today, are by now catalogued, appraised, analyzed, and museumed as decorously as the work of the Venetian and Flemish painters. Indeed, with much of modern art it is hard to decide whether it is serious art or, as the current jargon would call it, a "put-on."

We see, therefore, that cultivation of the aesthetic in schools depends on the roles of the three types of art: serious classical, serious avant-garde, and popular. With respect to the first two, some tuition is virtually indispensable; with respect to the last, tuition of any kind is probably unnecessary. Now if the arguments in behalf of cultivation have been at all persuasive, then it seems reasonable to reserve formal instruction for the serious arts. For even if our analysis of the relative superficiality of popular art is false, it still remains true that it is perceived and enjoyed almost spontaneously by those who live in the milieu in which it is exhibited.

One might say that to appreciate popular art is part of the general socialization process. Adolescents who do not know and like the Top Twenty tunes or who are unfamiliar with the popular images of femininity or masculinity in fashion, speech, and general life style are maladjusted — in the eyes of their peers, to say the least, and for an adolescent this is to say everything. The current crop of movies and television programs are almost necessary viewing if one is to converse with one's fellows on the job or in the taproom or the beauty parlor. The popular arts, therefore, for good or evil, are among the most potent means of social stability and control; they are the mores translated into aesthetic images. The common people — and we are all common people outside our fields of cultivation — abide by the aesthetic version of the mores as they abide by the moral version of them; they do not question them; they serve as inarticulate but powerful standards of right and wrong.

It was ever thus, one might argue — the elites enjoying the fruits of their cultivation and the *hoi polloi* regaling themselves with popular art. Why should it be different now? One answer is that in previous eras the power of the *hoi polloi* was strictly limited; what they enjoyed aesthetically made little difference because their economic and political power was virtually nil. Today this is no longer the case. Economic and political power either is or can be in the hands of the masses; they are the major culture consumers, and the forms of their feeling adumbrate their action. They no longer have to ask the elites what is proper to like or dislike; they make their own standards by rewarding the artists they favor and neglecting those who do not strike their fancy. It would be strange if the arts did not respond to this new fact of social life.

Just as it is dangerous to entrust the life of the nation and the world to citizens ignorant of good science and technology, so is it dangerous to entrust it to men and women whose feelings and values are uncultivated and undisciplined. This is the overriding reason for the cultivation of the young in the aesthetic dimension of experience. For a good society there must be enlightened cherishing.

EPILOGUE

Enlightened cherishing, serious art, aesthetic perception, and aesthetic education — how are they related to each other? It is time to bring them together.

From what has been said, it may now be clear, or at least persuasive, as to why the perceptual approach to aesthetic education seems to be the most viable one. The performance approach will not provide the universal cultivation of feeling. The standard appreciation approach leads to a superficial conventionalism, and it tends to stop at the frontier, where the tradition is no longer authoritative. Yet it is from frontier experimentation that the new behavioral forms of the classic virtues and values will emerge, not in the repetition of classical art or even the appreciation of it, and certainly not in the popular arts. We have no way of *knowing* which of the current experiments will throw up images of courage, manliness, womanliness, heroism, and patriotism which can capture the imagination of the coming generation, but if we cannot perceive aesthetic images with facility, then we shall have to wait fifty years before the imagination of the artist begins to affect the mass public. Our times are too fluid and too restless to permit us that much delay in responding either to frontier science or to frontier art. Yet whether the art is popular or serious, classical or experimental, the proper mode of perceiving is fundamental.

Without induction into the great heritage represented by the classical tradition, we are at the mercy of every bizarre vagary. We live in an age when producing novelty for the sake of novelty, and the profits that go with it, form an established industry. It has been said that there is no more avant-garde because of the rapidity with which the new is deliberately made obsolescent. The frontier should be the frontier of an established, highly organized hinterland; where all is frontier, nothing is really new.

There is no use abusing the stereotyped thinking and feeling of the establishment or the middle class or the blue-collar class. Every society lives by its stereotypes; they are the bread and butter of social life, the basic nutrition on which the social order sustains itself. By them society makes clear what it expects from its members and what the members can expect of each other. An experimental society — one in which everything is open to trial and retrial — cannot exist. The good society, like the good life for the individual, involves examining the stereotypes and not merely rebelling against them, and this examination is carried on by cultivated persons — buffs in thinking, feeling, and perceiving — connoisseurs who use the critical tradition to move forward to new ground. This is the enlightened life.

If the school takes these considerations seriously, it will provide a twelve-year continuous experience with aesthetic education, so that aesthetic literacy will be as common as the linguistic kind. This trend might be accelerated if we realized that the audiences for the serious arts are made up pretty largely from the ranks of college students and college graduates. The university or college today is the new seedbed of the arts, both for artists and for their publics. Not only do these institutions offer courses in the arts but they bring the very best art, old and contemporary, to the campus.

Can serious art survive on the patronage of so small a portion of the population? It is clear that in this country it cannot; every large cultural art enterprise is in economic straits despite large attendance and private gifts. The answer is a national subsidy, but this would be more gracefully justified if the bulk of our people, not only an exclusive minority, could enjoy them. But until the public schools take aesthetic education seriously, no such large public for serious art can come into being. It has been said that the twenty-first century may be the century of the masses. This will mean, one dares to hope, that enlightened cherishing, once the privilege of the few, can become the heritage of the many — of all who care to exert the effort to become connoisseurs of art, of life, and of value.

Index

117